THE SAINTS OF BREWSTER
1856-1996

By Paul F. Saint

Brewster, Massachusetts
Copyright 1996

This book is dedicated to my wife, Marion.

Table of Contents

PREFACE

In tracing the 140-year history of the Saint family in Brewster, Massachusetts, I have relied on my own memory (trustworthy as far back as the late 1920s), my father's memory (which reached back to about 1885), and on stories that have been passed down to us through family traditions and memoirs. I cannot vouch for the complete veracity of these stories, but I do feel that most of them have been validated by tradition, family remembrances, and stories told to my father by his mother and grandparents.

To the best of our knowledge, 1856 saw the first Saint appear in Brewster. Since that time, 140 years ago, the Saint family always has had a presence in Brewster. As of 1996, my wife and I own our own home at Saint's Landing on Robbins Hill Road, and our son Jack and his wife, Karen, own a summer home at Ocean Street on Winslow Landing in Brewster.

The Vital Records Office of the town of Brewster, the 1860 Federal Census for Brewster, and the town assessor's records have all been most helpful. Thanks to Janine Perry, archivist for the town of Brewster, for reviewing with me much of Brewster's history, including the real estate valuation list. (It was interesting to see that in 1862 Saint's Rest had an assessed value of only $20, while the Cow of the Saints had an assessed value of $30 as it was considered "income-producing" property.) There are many other people I should thank for helping me write these memoirs, starting with my oldest son, Mike, who (along with his brother Jack) helped me get the computer with which this book was written and who also spent many hours helping me edit and polish my ideas and memories. Bob Amerson was the one who gave me the final "push" to write. Bill Nielsen, president of the Brewster Historical Society, often discussed with me the history of the town. Robert Larkin, a member of Immaculate Conception Church in Brewster, supplied much material about Holy Trinity Church Cemetery. His father, Daniel Larkin, was a good friend of my father's back in the 1920s. Thanks also go to Greg O'Brien, former editor of the *Cape Codder*, for his excellent ideas, and to Jack Ahrens, whose creative writing course at Snow Library in Orleans gave me some valuable tips. I just hope I have used some of his splendid ideas.

Thanks to my wonderful wife who put up with hour after hour of my information gathering, writing, rewriting, editing, and polishing. Many thanks to the Good Lord for giving me more than 75 years of life to experience these events and the mind to remember them so I can share them with others.

If I have forgotten to mention family members or friends who have assisted me, I ask forgiveness for the oversight. I only hope that this life history of Paul F. Saint and the memoirs of my dad (who was born over 50 years before I was) will help all who read this autobiography recall some of their own memories of events which I have overlooked.

A note to my descendants: Please don't make the same mistake I made by waiting until you are more than 75 years old to write your memoirs. Hopefully, this book will help motivate my sons and grandchildren to write their memoirs, so that more than 100 years from now someone can write the 250-year history of the Saint family in Brewster—truly "God's Country."

PROLOGUE

Over 200 years ago, in August 1787, Edward Saint was born to John and Ann Saint in the small village of Crewkerne, Somerset County, England. As Edward reached maturity, he became a cordwainer (shoemaker) and married a woman named Frances Tyrell, of South Petherton, England, on June 19, 1812. Frances gave birth to six children, some of whom died at an early age, and died herself at the age of 30 on June 6, 1823. Three years later, Edward Saint wed again, marrying Sarah Harris of Wales, who was, like her husband and her father, a cordwainer.

Six children were born to Edward and Sarah Saint between 1827 and 1838. The third child was named Thomas Roach Saint (the same name, incidentally, given to the first child of Edward and Sarah Saint, a son who had died nine months after he was born).

In October 1989, my wife, Marion, and I-spent two weeks in the area of England where the Edward Saint family had lived, in the small town of Lopen. Lopen was once famous as the sailcloth-making center of England, especially in the days when Lord Nelson, the victor of Trafalgar, was an admiral in the Royal Navy. After several days of research, Marion and I found the cemetery of All Saints Church in Lopen where Edward Saint was buried.

We also discovered, in the small neighboring town of South Petherton, the chapel where my grandfather, Thomas Roach Saint, was christened—the Round Well Street Independent Chapel. It is no longer a chapel, having been purchased many years before by a wealthy businessman, who converted the chapel into an institution much like the Brewster Council on Aging and named it after his only son, David, who had died in an automobile accident.

On the day we visited David's Hall, we ran into an interesting situation. A woman was conducting a watercolor painting class for South Petherton senior citizens, the same kind of volunteer work that Marion did every Monday morning with elderly Brewster for over eight years. "What goes round comes around."

In the mid-1850s, Thomas Roach Saint, tiring of his father's cordwaining trade, shipped off to America to seek his fame and fortune. History tells us that the most common exit ports at that time were Liverpool and Southampton, but we have never learned from which Thomas Roach sailed.

My father, Thomas Edward Saint, always said his mother had told him that his father had been shipwrecked off the coast of Brewster on Massachusetts' Cape Cod peninsula. In the mid-1850s, according to contemporary Cape Cod newspapers, shipwrecks occurred two or three times a day, especially in the winter months. Many of these so-called shipwrecks were really instances of ships' running aground on the Brewster flats, since many sea captains were unaware of the area's extremely low tides. Moreover, "mooncussers" often hung lighted oil lamps from the necks of mules and walked the animals along the beaches at night hoping to trick ships into mistaking the mules for lighthouses, thereby causing wrecks from which they could scavenge cargo. Many Cape Cod natives used to "cuss the moon" when it was full, because its light disrupted their practice of causing shipwrecks. Mooncussers continued their activities into the 1920s during Prohibition, when they scavenged for whiskey. My brother, Tom, used to live on Mooncusser Lane, which derived its name from these same mooncussers.

Whether he arrived by shipwreck or by more conventional means, by 1860 Thomas Roach Saint had arrived on Cape Cod: The 1860 Federal Census for Brewster lists him as living at the home of Freeman Cobb in Brewster, for whom he worked as a gardener and laborer.

Freeman Cobb lived with his wife, Annette (who was also his first cousin), their small children, and two Irish maids in a big home on the northern side of Main Street (Route 6A), just east of the Brewster Lutheran Church and west of the famous Brewster Village Store.

Freeman Cobb made his money in the stagecoach business in South Africa and Australia. Although he died in South Africa, a gravestone commemorates him in Brewster Cemetery on Lower Road, where his wife and children are buried.

Many of his family were sea captains and included his uncle, Captain Freeman Cobb, Sr., and the noted Captain Elijah Cobb.

The original Freeman Cobb home was dismantled in about 1950; and a new more modern home was built by the present owners, Hank and Barbara Allen, direct descendants of Freeman

Cobb. The original barn is still standing on the property, east of the new home.

In the same period that Thomas Roach Saint was emigrating to America, other ancestors of ours were working as tenant farmers in Ireland. William Starkey, my great-great-grandfather, appears in the Tithe Applotment Records as a worker on a farm for the Lord Viscount of Lismore in the Township of Glincallihan, near Clogheen, County Tipperary, Ireland. A little later, the name of Peter Starkey, my great-grandfather, appears in the Griffith's Valuation Records as a tenant farmer for Edmond Hyland in the small Township of Scart East, two miles from Clogheen.

In the early 1850s, Peter Starkey and his three oldest children left for America, where they started an asparagus farm in Chatham, Massachusetts, also on Cape Cod. His wife, Alice Starkey, accompanied by their three youngest children and his father, William Starkey, followed them, arriving in Boston on May 31, 1854, aboard a ship named the *Meridian*.

The Starkey family was the first Catholic family to settle in the town of Chatham, living on Highland Avenue, near the present location of a Catholic church. When the Starkeys, including daughter Ellen, moved to Brewster, they built a home on Robbins Hill Road, directly across the street from where Marion and I now live.

In 1867, the Holy Trinity Catholic Church of Harwich paid $225 to an Obed Brooks for four acres of land on what is now Route 124 for a cemetery. The deed was filed on January 28, 1868. Another section was purchased in 1920.

In early 1868, my great-great-grandfather William Starkey (my father's maternal grandfather) became one of the first people to be buried in the Holy Trinity Church Cemetery. He was followed in later years by my great-grandparents, Peter and Alice Starkey, and, in 1872, by my grandfather Thomas Roach Saint.

CHAPTER ONE

THE ELEVEN-YEAR MARRIAGE OF THOMAS AND ELLEN (STARKEY) SAINT (1861-1872)

The 11 years Thomas Roach and Ellen (Starkey) Saint spent together must have been extremely harsh ones, judging by the stories from my only sources—my father and occasionally Aunt Nell.

My grandfather Saint (who died 47 years before I was born) was, as noted, a poor immigrant from England, who made a meager living by farming and working as a landscaper for the sea captains of Brewster. He operated a small farm and owned a cow, a horse and wagon, a flock of chickens, a rooster, and other small animals.

My grandmother Saint (who died 12 years before I was born) was quite a woman. She was tiny—under five feet tall and weighing less than 100 pounds—but of great capacity. After arriving from Ireland in 1854, she worked as a live-in maid in Chatham and Brewster in the homes of wealthy sea captains and successful merchants.

An Irish immigrant who practiced the Roman Catholic faith in towns that had few Catholics, she married an Englishman who had been christened in a nonconformist chapel. After four or five years of married life, Thomas converted to Catholicism, largely because his wife Ellen's fine example.

Although I have seen several photographs taken in the early 1900s of my grandmother Saint, neither I nor my relatives have been able to find any pictures of my grandfather Saint. Perhaps a picture is lacking because he died in 1872, when little was known of photography, or perhaps because the Saints could not afford to hire a photographer.

Young Ellen Starkey, who was working as a domestic in Brewster, met young Thomas Roach Saint, the gardener in the home of Freeman Cobb. The couple fell in love and were married on April 28, 1861, in Sandwich, the only town on Cape Cod that had a Catholic church.

They moved to Robbins Hill Road to live in Saint's Rest, first as a tenant of Ellen's father, Peter Starkey, and later bought the house for $90.

The Saints lived mostly off the land and the sea. Even though all historians seem to agree that the rocks, salt, and sand in Brewster would not be too conducive to farming, my grandfather worked long hours cultivating and maintaining his small farm. The family consumed most of the produce of their large vegetable garden and sold the rest to neighbors. They fished and clammed in Cape Cod Bay, and their catch included herring, which they hung up to dry in the barn.

It must have been a desolate life for them, especially during the harsh winter nights spent way out on the hill at Robbins Hill Road, with the northeast winds howling through the poorly insulated house. The only heat was provided by a wood stove, a small fireplace, and a kerosene oil cooking stove that gave off some warmth when the oven door was left open.

My grandmother Saint was, I understand, an excellent cook who canned tomatoes, beach plum and grape jelly, and other products for the cold, cruel winters this poor family faced.

In their brief 11 years of married life, Thomas Roach and Ellen (Starkey) Saint had seven children: Sarah, William, Mary, Ellen, Thomas (my dad), Alice, and Peter (born a few months after his father's death).

SARAH

Sarah Saint, my aunt and the oldest child of Thomas Roach and Ellen Saint, was born on March 3, 1863, in Brewster. She married Henry McDade, and she died in Lawrence, Massachusetts, around 1950. The McDades had seven children: Lola, a piano teacher, who had to have her leg amputated because of a serious infection one summer in Brewster; Josephine, a schoolteacher who never married; Marie; Miriam, who, tragically, died near Thanksgiving Day, two days before her planned wedding; sons Henry and William; and the youngest child, Edna (McDade) Powell, who, while in poor health in 1996, is still alive and living in the Midwest.

WILLIAM

William Peter Saint, the oldest son, was born December 30, 1864. He worked for the New York and New Haven Railroad for many years as a baggage agent in Hyannis. After retiring, he became an insurance agent for the Travelers Insurance Company.

Uncle Will married Carrie Skinner Holmes on January 17, 1894, in Hyannis, Massachusetts. She was the daughter of Allen Gorham Holmes and Cynthia Landers (Lumbert) Holmes, with a direct lineage to Elder William Brewster, John and Priscilla Alden of the Mayflower, and Samuel Rider, "The Migrant" of Yarmouth. As Carrie's father was the sexton at the Hyannis Baptist Church, she was allowed, as a small child, to ring the church bell by swinging on the rope. Uncle Will and Aunt Carrie had no children and lived in Hyannis their entire married life. Uncle Will died on March 30, 1951, and Carrie died on May 27, 1962.

MARY

Mary E. Saint (whom we all called "Aunt Maime," sometimes spelled "Mame") was born on October 2, 1866, and died on February 24, 1929, at the Cape Cod Hospital in Hyannis. Aunt Maime married David Henry Sears. D.H., as everyone called him, was born in Brewster on Stony Brook Road in what is (in 1996) the Packet Antique Shop. Aunt Maime and Uncle David Henry Sears had two daughters: Gertrude (Sears) Hodsdon, who died in 1997 at age 93; and Mary "Molly" (Sears) Doherty, who lives in western Massachusetts. Molly had five children and Gertrude three, including former East Dennis Postmaster Bill Hodsdon.

D.H., Aunt Maime, Gertrude, and Gertrude's three children operated a wonderful bakery and ice cream parlor in East Dennis on Cape Cod for many years.

ELLEN

Ellen "Nell" Beatrice (Saint) Sears was the fourth child of the Thomas Roach Saints. She was born November 26, 1867, and died at age 91 on October 9, 1959. Aunt Nell married Thomas Walter Sears, brother of David Henry Sears. Uncle Walter and Aunt Nell were a remarkable couple—married happily for over 60 years, despite the fact that she was an ardent Roman Catholic and he a Protestant.

I remember well how every Sunday Uncle Walter would drive Aunt Nell to Mass at the Immaculate Conception Catholic Church in East Brewster, sit out the service in his car reading the Sunday newspapers, and then drive her home.

Uncle Walter owned and operated a meat market in East Dennis. Every few weeks in the summer Uncle Walter and Aunt Nell would entertain us at their home on Main Street in East Dennis, which was directly opposite present-day Sears Road. Aunt Nell was a marvelous cook and would entertain my mother, my brother, and me with samples of her famous blackberry grunt, while Uncle Walter would entertain my Dad with a "snifter" of whiskey—about one ounce in a small glass with no ice, soda, or anything else to spoil the drink. A few weeks later, the Sears clan would visit our house in Brewster for a "return engagement."

Uncle Walter and Aunt Nell had six children: Issac, Walter, Cedric, Madeline, Beatrice, and Ellen. Isaac died quite young, and I can't say that I even remember him. Walter Roy Sears sold gloves. Cedric "Ted" Sears married Ruby Tyler, a nurse, who helped me out considerably with the research she had done on the Sears and Starkey families. Madeline became a nun in the Order of the Sisters of Saint Joseph, taking the name of Sister Thomasine after her beloved father. She was stationed for many years at St. Aidan's School in Brookline, Massachusetts. Unfortunately, at age 50, she became quite ill and died in Framingham, Massachusetts.

The fifth child was Beatrice (Sears) Silver, who married George Silver.

The youngest child born to Uncle Walter and Aunt Nell was Ellen (Sears) Curran, who married a David Curran from Boston. Both Dave and Ellen were educators, she a teacher and he an administrator. Ellen was the first person baptized in the Immaculate Conception Church in East Brewster and was a staunch Catholic all her life. She was a daily communicant and was considered by many of us as a "living saint." In all my life I never heard anyone say a bad word about her, nor did I ever hear her say a bad word about anyone else. She died peacefully in her sleep in 1994. May she rest in the peace she so richly deserves.

THOMAS

My father, Thomas Edward Saint, was the fifth child and the second son of Thomas and Ellen (Starkey) Saint. He was born on February 15, 1869, and died on October 19, 1955, in Brookline, Massachusetts. He married Mary (Kelly) Saint on October 19, 1910, in Boston. Much more will follow about my fabulous father.

ALICE

Alice Cecelia (Saint) Howes was born in 1871 in Brewster. She was not only my aunt, but also my godmother. I don't really remember her, as she died when I was only two years old. Alice married G. Knyvet Howes of Brewster. She was the second of three wives for Knyvet, and they had no children. They   lived in a nice home on the south side of Main Street (Route 6A)—the nearest house in Brewster to the Brewster-Dennis line.

Alice is buried in the small Sears Cemetery right behind their home. She qualified to be buried there since Knyvet's mother was a Sears.

PETER

Peter R. Saint was born on January 11, 1873, several months after his father's death, and died on March 29, 1957, in Brockton, Massachusetts. Uncle Peter was with the *Brockton Enterprise* newspaper as a linotyper for over 40 years. He married Gertrude Peters, and they had two children—John "Gus" Augustine, who died in 1982, and Helen (Saint) Provost, who is still living in 1996 and residing in Pelham, New Hampshire.

"Gus" Saint used to come to our home in Brighton quite often for dinner while he was at Boston University's night school. At age 45, Gus finally married, and he and his wife had one daughter. He worked at the famous Wayside Inn in Sudbury, Massachusetts, until a tragic fire destroyed the inn. Later, he was let go by the Ford Foundation, which operated the inn. Helen, too, did not marry until middle age, and she and her husband had no children.

All the children of Thomas Roach and Ellen (Starkey) Saint inherited their parents' strong character traits, including willingness to work. In the early days of married life for Thomas and Ellen, all of their children, out of necessity, helped out in any way they could to bring some money into the home. Some did light housekeeping, and some helped other families take care of their babies. When the older Saint children were ages six to nine, they began to help their mother with the care of the garden, and with the pigs, hens, and cow. They also collected "poverty grass" and sold it to neighbors at 25 cents a bushel (poverty grass was used to kindle fires in the fireplaces).

As a young girl, my Aunt Nell followed in her mother's footsteps and did housework for the same Freeman Cobb home in Brewster where her father had worked as a gardener and laborer when he first came over from England. Aunt Nell also worked as a domestic in the home of Mrs. L.M. Crowell.

It is interesting to note that, despite the horrible conditions in which the Saints lived, all seven children (except for Aunt Alice, who died at age 50) lived until well over 70.

CHAPTER TWO

YEARS OF SURVIVAL (1872-1907) AND THE AUTOBIOGRAPHY OF THOMAS E. SAINT

1872-1907, YEARS OF SURVIVAL

Thomas Roach Saint was ill only three days before his death from what they called "dropsy." When my grandfather Saint died, in the winter of 1872, his body was transported by horse and buggy 35 miles to the Catholic church in Sandwich. It was an overnight trip, and the next day, after a funeral Mass in St. Peter's Church (now called Corpus Christi Church), the funeral procession took the long 35-mile trip back to the burial site at Holy Trinity Catholic Cemetery on Route 124 in Harwich Center. Then, it was back to the "Old Homestead" on Robbins Hill Road in Brewster.

With no heat in the house, the oldest child aged nine, no father to help support the family, and only $300 left to feed the family of seven (soon to be eight), the Saints must have really been in dire straits.

Several months after the death of Thomas Roach Saint, Peter, the third son and seventh child, was born. At the same, the Mullin family next door also had a baby boy, Daniel. Unfortunately, Mrs. Mullin died at childbirth, so Ellen Saint breast-fed the Mullin baby as well as her own. She went on to raise Daniel Mullin along with her seven children. (A hard story to believe; however, not only my father, but also my Aunt Nell and her son, Ted Sears, corroborated the story.)

The oldest child, nine-year-old Sarah, and her younger brothers and sisters all pitched in to help support their mother and family. My own father, Thomas Edward Saint, often told me stories about how he and the rest of the family survived. Both my uncle Will Saint and my dad helped by fishing, clamming, working in cranberry bogs, and other ventures to earn some money for their mother.

Ellen (Starkey) Saint died in Brewster of cancer on March 8, 1907. She had "run the good race," and was buried beside her husband and with her father, mother, and grandfather in the Holy Trinity Cemetery on Route 124 in Harwich. Ellen Saint was aged 71 at the time of her death and had outlived her husband by 35 years. May she rest in peace.

AUTOBIOGRAPHY OF THOMAS E. SAINT

Thomas Roach Saint was quite a man, the only one of 12 children who left the trade of cordwaining in England to emigrate to America—with no idea of what he was going to do once he got there.

My father's autobiography vividly describes his early days. He quit school in the third grade (as did the noted Cape Cod author Joseph Lincoln, who was in the third grade with my father). The Brewster Grammar School was then located in a small building on Main Street near Swamp Road. Later, the school was converted into a plastics factory.

My father used to tell me that his two brothers also quit school early to take part-time jobs to help their mother. His four sisters stayed in school a little longer than their brothers, but worked part time in any capacity they could.

I can recall quite vividly the tremendous fear of guns (even toy ones) that my father always had—especially when we brought our little sons with their toy guns over to visit him. It must have been years until I found out the real reason for my father's fear of weapons. It seems that when my father was in his teens, he took his younger brother and a friend out shooting ducks on Cape Cod Bay. Unfortunately, my uncle's gun went off prematurely, and his friend was killed.

THE AUTOBIOGRAPHY OF THOMAS EDWARD SAINT, BORN FEBRUARY 15, 1869. Written in 1954—a year before he died at age 86.

Father died after three days' sickness, leaving my mother with seven children, the oldest being 10 years of age. All we had was 300 dollars and our 250-year-old home, part of which was built by one of the Robbins family who came over on the Mayflower. All this shore was named after him.

My good mother always said to us that it was no disgrace to be poor, but a terrible disgrace to be dishonest. At eight years of age, I made my first money. My good mother had not a dollar in the world at this time, and I knew that I could get some money for her. So, when the tide went out one day, I took a long cord and a pitch fork. Then, out I went. In April, the water is "darn" cold to catch flounder, but it did not mean a thing to me. I wanted to get those fish and sell them, and you bet I did. I caught 150 of them, cleaned them, and went to the main part of town where I sold them for three cents apiece. So, that day, I took $4.50 home. I called first on the Rev. Mr. Hawes, a minister, and he said, "My boy, how old are you?"

"Eight," I said.

"Why are you selling fish at your age?" he asked.

"My poor mother has no money," I replied. On the following Sunday, this good man, from the pulpit, told his people about this boy eight years of age. He said, "When he comes to your house, always buy from him."

In a few days, I dug clams, cleaned them, and up I went to sell them. I sold them all in two hours and made three dollars. Of course, my brother helped me to clean the fish and clams. I only wish that there were more men in the world like Rev. Mr. Hawes.

During our childhood, we had a good time with our toys, which consisted of apples, turnips, etc. Now, children have new toys every other day. Expensive ones, too. We still had a lot of fun with what we had.

That March when I was nine years old, I made molasses candy and popcorn, and bought a half bushel of peanuts. I took them up to the Town Meeting and was sold out before two o'clock. That day, I made four dollars for my good mother.

In April, Postmaster Knowles asked me if I would like to carry the mail from the post office to the houses along the road. Each house would give me sixteen cents a month, which amounted to a little over 60 dollars each year. Gee, but I felt rich. I was the youngest ever to carry government mail in America. I would get excused from school at 11:30 a.m. until 1:30 p.m. and eat my lunch along the road. I worked at that until I was 14 years old. Then, my brother had the job for two years.

I worked around cutting lawns, gardening, and weeding cranberry bogs. At 16, I went to work driving an order cart for a grand old man, Mr. Warren Lincoln, who ran a general store. I made $10 a week and also worked in the store until 10 each night.

At 19, I got a job to work at Monument Clubhouse in Bourne at Buttermilk Bay. I would report March 15th, and work until October 1st. That job paid $300 each season. You can imagine how rich I felt.

The first thing I had to do was to was help Captain Phinney. He and his wife had charge of the Cliff House. They always had a freight car of liquor from S.S. Pierce, which is some job to put away in the cellar. These men had leased both sides of the Monument River, which is now the Cape Cod Canal. They always stocked it with trout after the April 1st fishing season began. I would go along with these men when they would go fishing and hold the basket of fish.

We always had a bottle of whiskey with us, and every time the men would catch a fish, I would give them a drink. When it was time to go home, some of the men would ask me, "Tommy, how many fish did we get?" Sometimes, I would say, "Three or four." But, how did they have so many drinks? I don't know.

That was in the year 1888. These men were the Hortons, Stackpoles, Bradlees, Windsors, Armorys, Minots—all very rich. In these days, they had a special train to go to Boston from Cape Cod. This train was called a "Dude Train" and only made three stops. It would leave in the morning at 10 a.m. and return in the afternoon at 3 p.m. Only these men could ride on this train. They had to pay three dollars each besides the regular fare, which amounted to about 40 dollars altogether. I would drive them to the station and call for them each day. I drove a team of white horses. These men had too much money, and all they thought about was eating and drinking—in *other words, their stomachs.*

At that time, President Cleveland had just married the most beautiful woman to ever come to Cape Cod. Other times, Joe Jefferson, the famous actor of Rip Van Winkle *fame, would come to the Club with the President and his beautiful bride for lunch. What a life. I worked for these men for three years. In the fall, I came home to Brewster, and we all picked cranberries. We made about $400.*

My good mother would then fit us all up for the winter with the money. She could make a dollar go farther than anyone I ever met. That winter I made up my mind that I was going out in the world and make money. As Henry Ford always said: "Sacrifice and hard work." That I have done since I was eight years of age.

In June of 1892, I told my mother that a young man whom I had gone to school with had a job in a well-known house in Boston. My mother said, "You watch out in the big city." So, off I went to Boston to see this young man, Daniel Mullin (the same young man that my mother had breast-fed along with my baby brother, Peter).

He took me down to Brown Durrell Company to see a great man at that time, Mr. T.B. Fitzpatrick. He looked me over and said, "Young man, you do not look to me like you would last one week at this work. The only job that I have is opening cases in the stockroom." It paid $5 a week, and I said that I would be pleased to have the job. He didn't know that I had been working on the cranberry bogs, wheeling sand, and digging ditches.

At that time, I only weighed 128 pounds, but every muscle was hard and strong. I started in 1892, and I am still working for the same company. It is now my 61st year with the company, and I will be 85 on my next birthday. I can still "lick wildcats."

I worked in the stockroom and waited on the trade when buyers would come in. I took my first trip on the road in 1897 with a Mr. Ed Simonds, a fine man from Vermont. He gave me some real inside on selling. After that I went out alone.

The first sale I made myself was at H.L. Goodwin's in Keene, New Hampshire. Mr. Goodwin was a wonderful man and a good friend. I arrived at his store at 11:30 a.m., stayed *there all day, and sold him $2,700 worth of merchandise. That was the largest order that anyone ever sold him in men's wear.*

From that time on, I traveled all over New England—every city and town. Then, I left for Michigan as far north as Mackinaw Island. From there, I came back and sold only the large cities 50 miles from Boston. I worked very hard, and my health gave out. So, I had to stop carrying heavy sample cases.

In 1914, I went to see Raymond's ("where you bought your hat") and met Mr. Frank Dorr. It took me about three months before I got his good will.

From then on, I could sell him the State House. In 1920, I had my biggest year. I sold him $375,000. Ever since, Raymond's has been Brown Durrell's biggest account.

Mr. Dorr passed away some years ago, and now the concern has done a wonderful business with Mr. Shaye and his two sons. They are "wonder men" in the department store business.

I never had a better friend than Mr. L.B. Haughey, vice president and general manager of Raymond's. The Brown Durrell Company is a wonderful concern, and they now have built a grand plant in Cambridge on Memorial Drive facing the Charles River.

In 1910, I married a very nice girl by the name of Miss Mary Kelly. She came from South Boston and was the daughter of Mr. and Mrs. Patrick Kelly, who were highly thought of in South Boston. Today we have two fine sons, Thomas and Paul, who are making good for themselves. We also have a summer home in Brewster which we call "Saint's Rest" and where we spend our summers.

Below is reprinted a eulogy for Thomas Edward Saint written by the president of Brown Durrell Company.

"In the passing of Tom Saint on October 19, 1955, Brown Durrell Company has lost one of its best-known and one of its most beloved members. He had reached the notable age of 86 years, and he also had the distinction of establishing the longest record in our entire history, of continuous employment for more than 63 years.

"Born in Brewster, Massachusetts, on February 15, 1869, he was always a most enthusiastic and patriotic champion of the beauties and attractions of his native Cape Cod, where he spent his youth and most of his vacations. As a boy, his resourcefulness in obtaining a variety of jobs helped to build a strong constitution and was a formative influence in the development of that aggressive enterprise which became so characteristic in his later success as a salesman. He began his career with our Company on January 26, 1892, and, as was the practice at the time, he spent the first five years of his apprenticeship learning the merchandise stocks and the principles of the business, by intensive application inside the plant.

In 1897, he became an outside salesman, and he continued in that capacity the rest of his life. One of his most outstanding characteristics was his almost constant cheerfulness, certainly a valuable asset in any salesman.

In addition to his success in business, Tom Saint also established a reputation as an exemplary family man and a widely respected citizen. He had an exceptional capacity for making friends; and in the hearts of all our members who had the privilege of knowing him, his ardent spirit, his vital generosity, and his intense loyalty will long be held and cherished in affectionate remembrance."

———————————————

My father was a "jobber" at Brown and Durrell—the middleman between the manufacturer and the retail store. He sold Gordon hosiery, ladies' undergarments, and Cape Cod shirts for men.

Over a 38-year period, my father rose from a warehouse man at five dollars a week to become a top salesman at $28,000 per year—big, big money in 1928. (In 1996 dollars, it would be about $280,000.) My mother had a full-time live-in maid for five dollars a week and a laundress for one dollar, one day a week.

When the Great Depression put the whole economy in a tailspin, my father lost everything: his stock in his company, stocks that he had bought on margin, and his sales manager job—he had to go out selling again.

Some men jumped off rooftops, and others faded away. My Dad, who had gone from rags in his childhood to riches when he was 55-60, went again from riches to rags; his income in 1933 was only 25 dollars a week. He went back to selling underwear and hosiery, took his sample case, and "hit the road." At age 86, he was making $20,000 a year on commissions and was still working the day he died.

When I graduated from Boston Latin School, he offered me all the money he had left for my college education—$200, that enabled me to get in the front door of college. I myself earned enough to get out the back.

I have never met another person who had more enthusiasm and pep than did my father. Having obtained only a third-grade education, he persevered and at age 30 received his high school diploma. He helped support his mother and six other siblings until they finished high school or secretarial school and then at 41 married my mother who was only 22. He died on their 45th wedding anniversary. May he rest in peace.

CHAPTER THREE

SAINT'S REST IN BREWSTER

Saint's Rest, a home on Robbins Hill Road in Brewster, was owned by my grandparents from 1861 to 1910, and thereafter by my parents, Thomas Edward and Mary J. (Kelly) Saint. In 1940, near the end of the Great Depression, my parents, in need of money, sold it to Dr. Joseph Rockett, a dentist from Newton, Massachusetts, and his wife. Upon the deaths of the Rocketts, their only heir, Mrs. Virginia Wellock, received ownership of the house. The Wellocks owned it until 1993, when they sold it to Mr. and Mrs. Martin Kaymarck of Washington, D.C.

Upon purchasing Saint's Rest, the Kaymarcks invested a lot of money in renovating and reconstructing the home and doing a wonderful job of relandscaping the grounds. The "new" Saint's Rest has four large, modern bedrooms—each of which has a view of Cape Cod. Saint's Rest originally was made up of parts of a few other homes—some elements having been transported across from Harwich.

When I was a boy enjoying my summers there, there were two steep stairways on the east and west sides of the house leading to four small bedrooms on the second floor. The architecture of the house was supposedly Grecian Revival, popular in the 1860s, but so much has been added to the house over the years that it's anyone's guess what the style of the house may be called now.

I remember the barn so well. My father always told me that the timbers came from the famous Brewster Salt Works which were located 500 yards west of Saint's Rest. Over the years, two bedrooms were built in the loft of the barn, and then an "in-house." The in-house (in contrast to an outhouse) was inside the barn, but the toilet hole was 10 feet above the dirt floor of the barn's basement. Later, plumbing was installed to provide "facilities."

A couple of years ago, one of my neighbors asked if all the reconstruction going on at Saint's Rest saddened me. I replied that I was delighted because Saint's Rest had never looked better.

CHAPTER FOUR

THE EARLY DAYS OF THE MARRIAGE OF THOMAS EDWARD AND MARY J. (KELLY) SAINT

Three years after his mother's death, Thomas Edward Saint, a 41-year-old bachelor (who had been selected by the *Boston Post* newspaper as the second-most-eligible bachelor in Boston—see attached photo), met a young colleen (Irish girl) by the name of Mary Kelly, of 778 East Broadway (between L and M Streets) in South Boston. Mary was called "Babe" all her life, even right up to her death in 1979.

She was the only daughter of Patrick J. and Mary (Dorr) Kelly and only 22 years old. As she was an only child, her parents had the resources for a private-school education at Notre Dame Academy on Granby Street in the Back Bay, lessons to ride horses (which she did quite well), and membership in dancing school. After high school, she attended Burdett College and later taught shorthand at Bryant and Stratton Secretarial School in Boston.

After a brief courtship, my father and mother were married in the Gate of Heaven Church in South Boston. My father used to tell people that his wife was the only person who entered the Gate of Heaven a Kelly and came out a Saint. A poor joke, but he just loved to tell it.

I can't remember all the names of the wedding party (as my mother told me years ago), but I do recall that a Judge Thomas Zanzibar Lee was the best man and that my mother's dearest friend, Margaret Gilbride (who later married a Dr. William Quigley of Charlestown), was maid of honor. Among the bridesmaids were Genevieve Giblin (who later married druggist Thomas Grimes of West Roxbury), Helen Walsh (my mother's cousin), Bessie Logan (daughter of General Edward Logan, of World War I fame), and Claire Pfeffer (who later married F. Lincoln Pierce, a lawyer from Newton).

For the first few years of married life, my father and mother lived in the Kellys' four-story brick home in South Boston, as my grandfather Kelly had suffered a severe stroke and was forced to sell his retail furniture store on G street in South Boston.

In 1916, after six years of childless married life, my mother gave birth, on September 7, to her first child, a son, my brother, Thomas A. Saint. Shortly thereafter, my parents moved (with the Kellys) to an apartment on Melton Road in the Brighton section of Boston.

Two and a half years later, on May 15, 1919, I was born—my parents' second and last child. My mother always told me that her obstetrician, Dr. Fred Good, came to deliver me in his tuxedo, as he had just left a big formal dinner honoring General John Pershing, of World War I renown. She also said that my brother, Tom, weighed eleven and a half pounds when he was born, and I weighed nine and a half. Who knows?

My date of my birth came into question in 1942, when I was trying to find my birth certificate to enlist in World War II. The Vital Records Office of the City of Boston found that my true date of birth (as they had registered it) was really May *14*, 1919. All my Social Security records list me as having been born on May 15, but my Army records and all records since 1942 list me as having been born on May 14. Until her dying day, my poor mother insisted that she was there on May 15 and the City of Boston wasn't, and, therefore, she would always celebrate my birthday on May 15.

After I was born, my parents bought a duplex house for our grandparents and ourselves at 55 Wallingford Road in Brighton, a few hundred yards away from our rental on Melton Road. The Saint family lived at that home until after my marriage in 1948, when they sold it and moved to apartments in Brighton and Brookline.

Before his marriage, my father was very active in civic and charitable organizations, including the Charitable Irish Society and in the Catholic Union of Boston. He served on the Brookline Board of Trade and became a Grand Knight of the Knights of Columbus Council 110 in Brookline. Until his death, my father was the oldest living Grand Knight in Massachusetts.

He was a great long distance swimmer (in fact, until he was 70 years of age he would swim long distances at Saint's Landing Beach in Brewster). In 1908, he and a companion swam out to the Boston Light, a distance of several miles. On the way back, his buddy had a cramp and went under a few miles from the Winthrop beach. My father pulled him back above water and towed him over two miles back to the beach. Even though there were several people standing on the beach, none ventured out to save the two swimmers. For that act of courage, my father received the prestigious Massachusetts Humane Society Medal for Bravery.

Back in 1916, my father was so thrilled at becoming a father for the first time that he bought a ship's bell at an auction and gave to the Immaculate Conception Catholic Church on Main Street in Brewster for its choir loft. The bell is still there today, but is mostly inactive, as the town building inspector ruled many years ago that the choir loft was unsafe and could not support both people and an organ. However, the original ship's bell can still be rung on occasion.

CHAPTER FIVE

THE EARLY YEARS OF TOM AND PAUL SAINT (1916-1929)

As Tom was almost three years older than I, his early childhood is only a slight memory to me. I remember that my parents told me he attended the Mt. Saint Joseph's Academy on Washington Street in Boston's Brighton section for the first three grades. It was a parochial school run by the Sisters of Saint Joseph and about a 15-minute walk from our house.

After attending the first three grades, Tom transferred to the local public school, the Alexander Hamilton Elementary School. I can't remember if the transfer was caused by Mt. Saint Joseph's changing from a coed school to an all-girls school (which it did later) or because my family felt it was better for Tom to attend a public grammar school. In any case the change was followed by some interesting events.

First, after having been in the fourth grade at the Alexander Hamilton School for only a few months, Tom was given a double promotion to grade five. Then, a few months later, Tom was stricken with a ruptured appendix and was out of school for a few months, missing the time the fifth grade spent on fractions. Even though Tom was a good student, graduating eventually with an MBA from Harvard Business School, he, to this day, has always had problems with fractions.

The earliest memories I have of my childhood are of often being sick in bed with pneumonia, the flu, or other lung ailments. Because of these illnesses and a very bad case of progressive myopia, my mother always claimed I was a "delicate child," and I was not allowed to attend school until I was ten. I guess she was wrong in her diagnosis, as I have lived so far to age 77.

I never did attend kindergarten or the first four grades of elementary school like all the other children in the neighborhood. Instead, my mother taught me at home, then brought in a private teacher when the task extended beyond her scope. Because I had been sheltered, I turned into a very shy and introverted child, and, believe it or not (as my adult friends don't), I was extremely bashful and never said much to anyone. Now my friends tell me I never shut up.

What a relief it was for me when our family doctor (and his "assistant," my mother) decided that at age ten I was now healthy enough to attend school. How happy I was when I left our house that first day of school and how sad I was when the unthinking principal put me in the kindergarten with all the little "kids." When recess came, I had enough brains to go to the principal and ask her how I could move to a higher grade. After a most fundamental four-question test on simple math and English, she agreed to place me in the fifth grade. Unfortunately, just as my brother never mastered fractions because he skipped the part of fifth grade in which they learned fractions, I found myself with no knowledge of drawing, penmanship, or music. To this day, I cannot carry a note (although I always wished I could sing), I can't draw, and my penmanship causes people to think I am a doctor.

Six months after entering grade five at age ten, I heard of the prestigious Boston Latin School, a public institution founded in 1635, and learned there was going to be a set of entrance exams given in the near future for entering its seventh grade. I once again approached our beloved Principal Tate with what I thought was a simple request but which, to her, was a complete surprise. I asked Miss Tate for permission to take the test, and she almost passed out. However, she reluctantly gave her permission, and so the next year, in the fall of sixth grade (my first complete year in school), I took the exams for Boston Latin and was accepted.

For the next six years, I received some of the most difficult and yet most effective education I have ever had. The only subject with which I had no trouble was math. I became the first student at Latin School to receive 100% in math consistently, almost without exception, throughout my school career.

At that wonderful institution, I received what I consider the finest training a school can give to a student: learning how to study. That scholastic training worked well for me throughout college and graduate school.

As the last year of the 1920s came into being, I found out that my good friend, next-door neighbor, and classmate in the sixth grade at Alexander Hamilton School, Edward Berkovitz, was also going to attend the Boston Public Latin School in the fall of 1930. Much to my relief and satisfaction, Ed and I would be classmates at the Boston Latin School (if we could survive the attrition rate over the next six years). The dropout or repeat rate was then running about 67%. Ed is still alive today in 1996 and is living about 50 miles away in Marion, Massachusetts. I hope to see him again at our class's sixtieth reunion on May 11, 1996.

————————————————

One Saturday morning, when I was about 12 years old, Ed Berkovitz and I decided to take a short cut through the city yards where all the public works vehicles were stored—about a five-minute walk from my house. In the yards, I was "kidnapped" by a group of young hoodlums from the other end of Brighton, who, I guess, had been seeing too many Wild West movies at the local cinema.

Four or five of these wise guys grabbed me, while Ed was too fast for them and ran home to tell his parents. In the meantime, the hoodlums tied me to a tree, gathered some branches and put them at my feet, and told me they were going to burn me at the stake. I was petrified. On the way home, Ed met a neighbor, Apthorp Heath, and told him of my plight. Mr. Heath called the police, who were at the scene within five minutes; but the hoodlums had flown the coop, leaving me still tied to the tree with smoldering branches at my feet.

We spent the rest of the afternoon with the police, who seemed to know who my assailants were. We visited the local theater, and when the lights were turned on, the police and I spotted the hoodlums, who were then arrested.

At Monday morning's court session, the judge of the Brighton District Court reprimanded the four for several minutes and warned them if they were ever caught doing this again, they would be sentenced to youth detention centers.

It was really no "big deal," but I had bad dreams about it for quite a time.

————————————————

After the vigorous training at Boston Latin School, it was always refreshing for me to spend all my summers in Brewster at Saint's Rest on Robbins Hill Road, where my father and his six brothers and sisters had been born and raised. The only summer that I did not spend the entire time in Brewster was in 1926, when my father (then at the height of his prosperity), took my mother, my brother, my maternal grandmother, and two cousins to Europe for a six-week tour. We boarded the SS *Ohio*, a steamer of the Cunard Line, and took the ten-day cruise to Cherbourg, France.   From there, we traveled by train to Paris, where we spent a few days sightseeing. Again by train, we traveled to Lourdes in the Pyrenees mountains of southern France, where we visited the famous shrine to the Blessed Mother.

I was only seven years old at the time, but I still remember most vividly the scene at twilight when pilgrims—hundreds and hundreds of them, all singing the "Ave Maria"—marched down from the mountains with candles that were sheltered by cardboard containers. Some used canes, others crutches, some were in wheelchairs—all bound for the baths at the shrine where Saint Bernadette had experienced the apparition of the Blessed Virgin. It was an inspiring sight, regardless of one's religion.   Then we took a train back to Paris, stopping on the way to visit the Shrine of Saint Theresa in Lisieux.

Unfortunately, I spoiled the rest of the trip for my family by contracting ptomaine poisoning in Paris, coming up with a 106- degree fever in the hotel. My mother sent for a Catholic priest, as she didn't think I had long to go. To her surprise, a young man with a bright blue coat and slacks came to our hotel room and identified himself as a Catholic priest. This was 1926, and in the United States all Catholic priests wore Roman collars and vestments (not quite like 1996). What my mother didn't know (until the French priest told her) was that the French government did not permit most orders of Catholic priests to dress in clerical garb on the streets of France.

Needless to say, I did recover, after spending six weeks in the American Hospital in Neuilly (a suburb right outside of Paris), where there were many American doctors. Thus ended our proposed six-week trip to Europe.

It wasn't until almost 20 years later that I took my next trip to Europe, this time on an all-free "vacation," including Africa, courtesy of the United States Army. While on a three-day furlough, I met Dr. Richard Dax, Jr., son of the doctor who had treated me back in 1926.

The first major league baseball game that I saw was between the Boston Red Sox and the New York Yankees on May 15, 1926. The Yankees had all the stars such as Babe Ruth, Lou Gehrig, Tony Lazzeri, Mark Koenig, Joe Dugan, Bob Meusel, and Earl Combs; but the Red Sox, with a bunch of no-names, nevertheless won that game. Fred Haney, the Red Sox third baseman, who later became manager of the St. Louis Browns, was the only player remembered by baseball fans. I do recall the Red Sox won in the bottom of the ninth inning, 3-2. What a thrill for a seven year old on his first trip to a major league game.

Thirty years later, on July 12, 1956, I took our oldest son, Mike, (also on his seventh birthday) to a Red Sox-Chicago White Sox game, and Mike had the thrill of a lifetime (as did I), seeing Mel Parnell pitch a no-hit, no-run game.

Even though I spent all my summers (except for two summers during World War II) in Brewster, it was not until the summer of 1926 that I personally recall some incidents and people from Brewster.

The Brewster Store was owned and operated by Henry Crocker, who was the Brewster postmaster under Republican administrations. One of our thrills as young nine and ten year olds, was to go to "Mr." Crocker's post office late in the day to wait for the mail to come in and, in the meantime, to buy penny candy.

Once Franklin Roosevelt was elected the country's president, he decided to clean out all the

Republican postmasters and replace them with Democrats. So, Henry Crocker received his "marching orders," as did many other Republicans. Once Henry heard the official word from the White House, he told people that if he couldn't keep his postmaster's position, he would not allow the government to use his building for a post office. The new democratic postmaster, Tom Ellis, was obliged to build his own post office up the street on Route 124 in the direction of Harwich.

The Brewster Village Store continues to thrive today as a country store. First it was a church, then a general store operated by W.W. Knowles, then a post-office/country store owned and operated by Henry Crocker, and then operated by the inimitable Donald Doane.

Donald Doane was a real Brewster "character." I remember well how Donald would greet you in June. Even though he hadn't seen you since the previous September, he would react to you as if he had seen you the day before yesterday. He was one of the few people I ever knew that would start his conversations in the middle of a sentence.

One day, a credit manager came in to inquire about the credit and integrity of a summer resident who wanted a loan. Donald said he didn't know the summer resident too well, but he did know that the resident didn't pay his bills and would "swipe" a few cigars when Donald wasn't looking. That was the end of this man getting the loan he wanted.

Later on, when we were older, we used to go to the Brewster train station at the corner of Underpass Road and Route 137 to meet the Boston train, which would drop off a few passengers and the mail each night except Sunday .

My father used to employ state "wards" to help him cut down dead pine trees and cart the rubbish away. It cost my Dad one dollar a day for their services, and they were well worth it. First, there was George Washington Cash (see attached photo of Tom, George, and me in front of Saint's Rest). I believe George was the first Afro-American that I had ever met, and he was a real "treat." He lived somewhere up in Punkhorn, an area in Brewster inhabited by people with low incomes; I never did find out just where. He would just show up early in the morning with his black metal lunch box and find out from my father what he wanted done.

After someone found George dead in his little shack up in Punkhorn, my father hired another state ward named "Ikey" Dunham Sears, a white man who was slightly retarded. My brother, Tom, who was then in his early teens, and Toby Broderick, a friend of his from Brighton (who later became an orthopedic surgeon), used to drive Ikey crazy by shooting-BB pellets at his backside as he was leaning over to pick up rubbish. Toby always let out an Indian-like yell, and poor Ikey would wonder who was shooting at him. Not a very nice thing to do, but teenage boys did not think of that in those days —nor do they today.

One of our pastimes in those days was walking out to the last bar of the Brewster Flats. My father always accompanied us and told us it was one mile and a half out to Captain Fred Young's fish weirs (see attached photo graph of the "bathing beauties" of the twenties). The water at low tide, as I remember it, was about three to four feet deep inside the weirs, which were alive with mackerel, crabs, and assorted other kinds of fish.

Weir fishing is a difficult chore. The weirs are made up of an inner and an outer net. Trees are implanted in the flats to act as a leader for fish to follow into the weirs themselves. The fish follow the "leader" of trees in the water, enter the open gate (about five or six feet wide), and then swim round and round in the outer weir. Next, they enter the inner weir through another five- or six-foot-wide opening and swim around in the inner weir. Although at high tide the fish could escape through the two gates to freedom, it's remarkable that they never (or rarely) do so.

The procedure was that Captain Fred Young (where he got the title, I don't know) and his helpers would drive a horse and wagon out from the shore with a rowboat in the wagon. Upon reaching the weirs, Captain Fred and his crew would take down the dory-type boat and enter-the weirs to take load mackerel and other fish into barrels on the wagon.

Sometimes Fred would enter the weirs barefooted and with extra-heavy khaki pants held up by suspenders. He would bravely walk about, and when crabs eventually took a nip out of his feet, he would kick them off with a loud yell, causing the children to laugh and laugh. When the barrels in the wagon were loaded to the gills, Captain Fred and his gang would head for shore where big trucks from the New Bedford fish markets would be waiting to buy the fresh fish.

Weir fishing was the only visible means of support these men had, except for profits from small vegetable gardens and from selling eggs-and milk. Weir fishing continued for many years until modern science and modern transportation drove the weir fishermen out of business.

In the late 1980s, weir fishermen like Steve Ellis came before the Board of Selectmen (of which I was a member) to ask for permits to erect weirs on the Brewster Flats. "What goes around comes around." If you visit Brewster, you should walk out on the flats at low tide and watch (but do not bother) the weir fishermen at work.

When Tom and I were in our teens, we were often taken fishing in the small ponds of Brewster and Harwich. For example, we would drive over Route 124 to the Brewster-Harwich line and rent a rowboat from Mr. Small for two dollars for the afternoon.

We would row out on Long Pond a short way and then carry the boat into a small pond called Greenland Pond. It was alive with pickerel and white perch, and we used to bring minnows (which we caught at Saint's Landing) for bait. It was funny that when Tom and I were youngsters, we never fished in the salt water; but when our sons were growing up, we would go exclusively saltwater fishing out in Cape Cod Bay in front of Saint's Rest.

At first, we would walk out on the flats at low tide and start casting for "blues" as the tide turned. Thereafter, we owned our first little 11-foot aluminum rowboat powered by a three-horsepower motor, and then graduated up to a 15-foot motor boat, and finally to a 19-foot motor boat. When my son Joe was about 16, he bought ten lobster traps and moored them off Sesuit Harbor in East Dennis. Those summers we had many meals of boiled lobster meat thanks to Joe.

In the 1920s, Tom and I played with Walter Young and Roland Taber (the latter still alive in 1996), who were Captain Fred's grandsons. My father's five cottages always had several nine-, ten-, and 11-year-old boys with whom we played games.

Also at this time in Brewster, a Captain Bragg and his wife operated a very nice inn and eating establishment in their home. Captain Bragg had earned his captaincy in the Merchant Marine by transporting soldiers to France in World War I. On many a summer Sunday my father would take us to the Braggs for a home-cooked turkey dinner at the amazing price of 75 cents per person.

Alan Ryone, a grandson of Captain Bragg, is still alive and active in Brewster affairs. Alan's mother, Cynthia Bragg, died several years ago.

In the 1920s, author and lecturer Helen Keller, famous for overcoming deafness, blindness, and dumbness, spent a few weeks at the Bragg house with her companion, Anne Sullivan.

A story concerning the Braggs that I remember quite well happened when I was a teenager. I was awakened one night by the State Police, who had come to summon my father to the Barnstable jail to bail out Captain Bragg. It seems that Captain Bragg and another Brewster citizen (whose name I will leave unmentioned) had had a severe argument. The other "combatant" had come after Bragg with a pitchfork, which Bragg quickly and ably took from his opponent and then finished him off with a right to the jaw. Since my father was a good friend of Bragg's, he was given the privilege of getting up the bond to bail out the captain.

Another event that I recall quite well happened during the last days of Prohibition, about 1930-1931, when the rumrunners were still "running" from the Coast Guard. My father would get the signal some foggy night that the rumrunners were being chased into Cape Cod Bay by the Coast Guard and had dropped all their cargo of Johnny Walker Scotch and other brands of English whiskey onto the sand flats to be picked up the next night, after they had outrun the Coast Guard. Unfortunately for the rumrunners, the Brewster townies had other thoughts on their minds and went out on the flats by Model T, by horse and buggy, and by "shanks mare" (on foot) to rescue the "loot."

According to the story, and I am not sure if it is true or not, on one such night a man cranked up his old Model T and drove out to the last bar to recover the whiskey. He loaded up with several burlap bags full of Johnny Walker, but then made the mistake of sampling one bottle before he came ashore. It was said that after sampling three or four drinks, he fell asleep and woke up to find the incoming tide sweeping in after him. It was so late that he had to wade and practically swim for his life, leaving the valuable Scotch whiskey and his Model T to be covered by the incoming tide. When he came back the next day at low tide, he had to bring a tow truck to get his car ashore. Captain Fred Young was an honorable man (all 250 pounds of him), and he vouches for the truth of this story.

A story from back in the 1930s is about a couple we knew, Big John Considine and his sister Clara. She ran the Considine House (which is now called the Brewster Inn and Chowder House on Route 6-A), and he operated the gas station, which was located just east of the inn. Clara used to serve wonderful Sunday dinners for about one dollar a person; and my family, as well as the Dowlings and many summer visitors, came for dinner many weeks.   Big John (and I can't tell you how big he was, but I remember that he weighed well over 250 pounds) would sit in his office for hours and keep a close eye on his gas station and its trade. How he missed one incident I will never know, but I assure you it did happen. It seems that my mother (who always said she was an excellent driver and never had an accident in 20 years of driving) maneuvered our family's 1931 Buick in such a way that it couldn't be moved forward or backward without scarring the car and ruining John's beloved gas tanks. John called on four or five of his big friends, and they bodily moved the car sideways with no damage to the car or to the gas tanks.

I recall my father's telling Tom and me about the famous Billingsgate Island off the shore at Eastham and Wellfleet. He told us that Billingsgate used to be a thriving community with a church, a Coast Guard station, and other buildings, until abnormally high tides sunk the island in the late 1800s. Hard to believe, but this story is true. If you are fishing with a power boat off the Billingsgate Shoals today, you can still see, at extremely low tides, the remains of Billingsgate Island.

My father would often point out to us how the salt works were operated at their location in West Brewster near Wing's Island. The owners would sink wooden pipes about two feet in diameter into Cape Cod Bay and then draw the water up by a complicated maneuver to pass through several vats, until evaporation left the last stop as pure salt. The salt works were a moneymaking proposition until modern science forced them out of business.

A story confirmed by Janine Perry, town archivist, and proven by an original letter in the Archives Room in the Council on Aging Building, shows how valuable the salt works were to the community. In 1814, according to this tale, a British ship, the *Spencer*, sat out in Cape Cod Bay, and the ship's captain, Commander Raggett, sent a letter to the Brewster Selectmen that he would destroy the salt works unless the town paid him a ransom of $4,000. None of the neighboring towns would help, but the citizens of Brewster raised the money and saved the salt works.

––––––––––––––––––––

A little Cape Cod ditty that Brewster natives used to recite went like this:
It looks like Rain, said Barney Paine;
How do you Know? said Obie Snow;
Tell by the Looks, said Briar Brooks;
It thunders Loud, said Joe McLeod;
It lightning's Sharp, Says Homer Clark;
Hold Your Tongue, says Grampa Young.

––––––––––––––––––––

In his 1984 book, *Catholicism on Cape Cod*, Father Harold Whelan states that in 1855 Father Moran (from Sandwich) used to say Mass at the home of Peter Starkey, my great-grandfather, both in Chatham and Brewster.

The book goes on to mention that many years later, in 1907, one of the most significant acts of Father George Maguire's administration was the building of a mission chapel in Brewster.

Father Maguire purchased land on Main Street in East Brewster and hired John Rooney of Boston as the architect. John Considine, Freeman Ellis, and Joseph Doyle (father of the late Brewster Selectman Larry Doyle), all parishioners, graded the church grounds. The first stone of the chapel was laid by Father Maguire in August 1907. Arthur Crowell, whose wife was a Catholic, made the altar free of cost.

As mentioned before, my first cousin, Ellen Saint (Sears) Curran was the first person christened in the Immaculate Conception Church, and Freeman Thomas Ellis and Delia Hawkins were the first couple to be married there.

In 1926, we lost our only surviving grandfather, Patrick J. Kelly, a retail furniture dealer, when he died at age 80. Our paternal grandparents, Thomas Roach and Ellen (Starkey) Saint, we never knew, because they predeceased us by many years. All we know about Thomas R. and Ellen was what we learned from our own father, although he seemed to remember very little of his dad, having been only three when his father died.

Our only surviving grandparent, Mrs. Patrick J. Kelly, was our only ancestor of German descent. Born Mary Ann Dorr in Boston, she had much of the German blood in her as her mother, Mary Ann (Gram) (Kratz) Dorr, was born in Baden-Freiburg, and her father, Nicholas Dorr, was born in Alsace-Lorraine, France. Alsace-Lorraine belonged to Germany from the end of the Franco-Prussian War to the end of World War I. Before and after (except during World War II), it belonged to France, though it was inhabited mainly by Germans.

My Gramma Kelly (sometimes called "Nana") did most of the cooking in our house and much of the sewing and other household chores, especially during the Depression, when we lost our full-time live-in maid, Mary Culkin, an Irish immigrant.

I remember vividly an incident from the summer of 1925, when my grandparents Kelly were taking care of Tom and me while our parents visited friends in Harwich: A tremendous tornado passed directly over our barn, and the first thing we knew the barn roof was carried 100 feet down to the south of us, landing in one of our fields. Nana Kelly, with her stoic German ancestry, didn't utter a "peep," while my Grampa Kelly kept puffing away on his pipe.

CHAPTER SIX

SIX YEARS AT BOSTON LATIN SCHOOL

As the 1930s began, I entered, with interest and trepidation, the heralded Boston Latin School. On opening day, our esteemed headmaster told us to shake hands with the boys on either side of us, because before we graduated, two of us would be gone. What a challenge!

My six years at the Latin School were filled with trying to jam six hours of homework a night into the three I had. It was like "robbing Peter to pay Paul," as some nights we would have to steal time from studying math to study Latin or French or German. In any case, I survived, even though my attendance record (because of cases of pneumonia and/or the flu) shows I was out of school an average of two months a year, until my senior year when I missed only a few days.

As I told my golfing partner (and classmate at Latin School), Chester Berry, just the other day, I had little time for extracurricular activities at Boston Latin. I was struggling to survive and finished about half way down in the class. Without knowing it, through all this drudgery, I learned "how to study," a skill that I used throughout my lifetime.

The rugged pace at Boston Latin made it such a pleasure to get back to Saint's Landing in Brewster each summer and renew my old friendships. Unlike some schools, Boston Latin did not give us a great deal of summer homework, although we did have to complete "small" tasks such as reading the Old Testament in its entirety and doing a book report on its every book.

One summer in the early 1930s, a group of us boys decided to form a baseball team. Included were my brother, Tom, and I; John Latham; Walter Young; Roland Taber; Amby Broughton (killed in World War II); the three Hooper boys, Tom, Fred, and Bob; Junior Lee (whose father owned Lee's Sea Grill, which is now called Laurinos); Nate Weber; and a few more townies like the Gage brothers, John and Ernest; and Bob Crowell (still alive in 1996). Since all but my brother, Tom, Amby Broughton, and I were true "natives" and not "wash-ashores" (people who may have lived in Brewster all their lives but were not born here, and thus are not considered true Brewster "natives" by the "born-in-Brewster" natives),

we played as a "town team." Our first and sometimes second, third, and fourth games were with the "summer folks" from the "ritzy" Brewster Park. Other games were played with the boys from Camp Monomoy (now Cape Cod Sea Camps) and some other so-called town teams from Harwich and Orleans.

Most of the games were played at the field in front of the present town office facilities on Main Street in Brewster, and others at Camp Monomoy and in Harwich and Orleans fields. It was a lot of fun and kept us out of trouble, but how good we were I couldn't tell you.

When I was 14 or 15, Captain Allen Bragg, who lived in a big colonial house at the corner of Lower Road and Robbins Hill Road (still standing today under the ownership of Jeff Hayes, a New York television producer), asked me if I would help him out with his sailing camp at Camp Wahtona in Brewster. If I did, he said, he would teach me how to sail (of which I knew little or nothing). Camp Wahtona was an all-girls camp, and for a 14-year-old male, the offer was "too good to refuse."

CHAPTER SEVEN

DAYS AT HOLY CROSS AND MY FIRST FULL-TIME POSITIONS (1936-1942)

After graduating from Boston Latin School in the spring of 1936, I secured my first part-time job (through my cousin Henry Smith, chairman of the Boston School Committee), in the Boston School Department's business office. It was not really an exciting job, mostly filing and being a "gopher" for the fine old ladies who worked there. However, the pay was good—$15 a week—and I was able to stay in Boston with my brother and my father during the week.

In the fall of 1936, my eye doctor, Dr. Fred Verhoff, told me that I should not go to the Massachusetts Institute of Technology, because of all the homework and the close-up reading. Instead, he recommended (and I hope that my Amherst alumni friends will take this as I received it) that I try to get accepted at a small "easier" school such as Amherst College in Northampton, Massachusetts. (Most of us realize that Amherst College is now considered a top-grade liberal arts college, and it is most difficult to obtain even consideration for admission.) In any case, my mother and I climbed into the family's favorite 1931 Buick and set off on the long five- or six-hour drive to Northampton.

After a two-hour drive along the old Worcester Turnpike (Route 9), we arrived in Worcester, and my mother casually said, "Why don't we stop at Holy Cross? I've heard some nice things about it, and it will save me lots of driving."

We turned up College Road and into Linden Lane. School had already begun. We boldly asked for an appointment with the dean of admissions. I had my records from Boston Latin School and the results of my College Board examinations. After about a half an hour of conversation, Father Cox, the dean, agreed to accept me as long as I didn't mind sleeping in the upper bunk of a three-man room on the fourth floor of the ancient O'Kane Hall.

Our only problem was that I had no clothes with me except what I had on my back. "No problem," my mother said. "I'll leave you here and send your father back with your clothes tonight" (plus the $200 which was needed for my first quarter's tuition, room, and board). And so my four-year college experience began.

Within a month, I had three jobs. I waited on table three meals a day for the grand sum of one dollar a day (serving 12 students at each meal) I was also a sports correspondent (on a stringer basis) with the old *Boston Post* newspaper. My third job was the best and most lucrative: selling reversible coats, white socks, neckties, tee shirts, etc.—everything the typical college bookstore sells today—door-to-door to students on campus.

Reversible coats were the best sellers and the most profitable. I bought them at the factory for $12 each and sold them for $17, saving the students $5 over the price charged at local retail stores. Many a fall I would sell 50 to 100 coats. All I did was wear a reversible my size, bring a swatch of colors with me and "guesstimate" what my customer's size should be. If I made a mistake, I would bring back another size the following week.

In those days—and my grandchildren and even my children will find this hard to believe—Holy Cross was run like West Point or Annapolis. We all arose at 6:30 a.m. and had compulsory Mass every day (except Tuesday; why Tuesday? I don't know). We had to be in our assigned seats before Mass started so that the young Jesuit scholastics could check us off on a record sheet. Those who missed Mass received a demerit, and those with too many demerits lost the privileges to be off campus until 11 p.m. on Saturday night, or to leave campus on the weekends.

After Mass came breakfast in Kimball Hall—all 1,000 of us. Grace was said by "Black Jack" Reid (Father John Reid, S.J., dean of discipline), who walked the balcony to make sure every student was behaving. After each meal, we waiters had an opportunity to eat ourselves, but under time constraints because we had to be at class before 9 a.m.

As classes adjourned for the morning at 11:45, we waiters had to rush down to the dining hall to get our table set up, put water on the table, etc. Then, after lunch, we waiters again rushed to eat and raced to afternoon classes, the first one of which began at 1:30 p.m.

Usually, unless you were pre-med and had lab, you were through class by 2:30 p.m. In the fall, I would rush to the football practice field and write a story to be sent down to the *Boston*

Post for publication. I was paid the royal sum of 30 cents a column inch for anything of mine that was published. For some reason, either because the paper had confidence in my writing or because someone did not do his job, not a line of mine was ever censored, rewritten, or wiped out during the four years I worked as a stringer.

After evening prayers and supper, we adjourned to our rooms, where we were checked in at 7 p.m. and again at 10 p.m. by our friendly Jesuit prefects, like the beloved Father Francis Hart, S.J., who always wished us a "God Bless" at 10 p.m. I guess I'm beyond any statute of limitations at this point and won't receive any demerits for confessing that most nights I might have been in my room for the 7 and for the 10 p.m. checks, but that in between I was on campus, not in my room!

Between 7 and 10 p.m. was a great selling time for me, and I canvassed the corridors of different dormitories selling my wares. I had a most receptive audience, as the students never minded taking a little relief from their studies to look at my sample cases and see what kind of ties they could buy for 75 cents each.

Obviously, this schedule did not allow too much time for study, but that's where my excellent Boston Latin School training came in handy. Latin School had taught me how to study and how to listen attentively in class and retain much of what I heard. I did try to study under the blankets because compulsory lights-out was 10 p.m., and it was strictly enforced. At exam time, of course, I cut down on my selling hours and spent much time hitting the books; and then in winter I had time to study during the time I used to spend covering football.

Because of the outstanding Latin School curriculum (I had taken the same math and Latin courses in my senior year at Boston Latin School as I took in my freshman year at Holy Cross), I received a 99 percent average in first-year math at Holy Cross and a 98 percent average in Latin. The only subject I had trouble with was religion because many of my other classmates had attended Catholic high schools, and I had previously attended only public schools

The summer after my freshman year, I worked as assistant paymaster at the Watertown

Boston Elevated Railway (now the MBTA). That job was interesting, as I worked from 11 p.m. to 7 a.m. and often gave the conductors the exact time and handed out their wages on pay nights. My pay was a magnificent $19 a week—a big raise from the previous year. The pay for my job in the summer after my sophomore year was $21 a week, when I worked for the same Boston Elevated on the same shift in its Park Square headquarters in downtown Boston

I was offered a full-time job after graduation as a sales trainee for the Burroughs Adding Machine Company if I attained some success selling on a door-to-door basis. So, after my junior year, I obtained a job as a sales trainee for the Fuller Brush Co. and sold brushes door-to-door in Boston's Hyde Park section. It was quite an experience. We had "motivating" sales meetings every Monday night, when we had to announce the previous week's sales results and to sing songs with lines such as "Pack up your brushes in your old kit bags and sell, darn you, sell." Corny, but effective.

I had no auto, so I would leave my sample case with a friendly druggist in Cleary Square in Hyde Park, and take the Boston El from Brighton to Hyde Park every day. On Friday nights, my father would let me take the family car out to my territory to deliver the brushes I had sold that week.

I made 50 to 60 cold calls a day, and it worked. I sold more Fuller hair brushes than anyone else in the office and met some very nice people. Some kindly ladies would invite me in for a sandwich and a cold glass of milk on hot days in July and August.

Even with summer jobs, I always had time to spend three or four weeks on my beloved Cape Cod at Saint's Rest in Brewster.

With World War II War clouds on the horizon, we all felt it wouldn't be too long before we were serving our country. In my senior year, what could have been a tragedy hit me on the one day we had off between the first and second semesters. It was a cold, rainy, sleety night; and a few of us ventured to walk down from Beaven Hall (now a Psychology Center), one plateau above Kimball Hall, to where the movies were being shown. With loafers on and no salt or sand on the sidewalk, I took a "header" down the stairs from the Fenwick plateau (next to the standing clock) to the bridgeway leading to what was then called Loyola Hall (long since renamed Carlin House). I honestly cannot remember much of anything for the next several days, except I knew that I was in the infirmary. Then, when my roommate Charley O'Connor and my good friend, Bill Dowling, noticed that something was wrong, they literally smuggled me out of the infirmary and brought me in Bill's car to the office of Doctor John Curran Sr. in Worcester. (Dr. Curran was my brother, Tom's father-in-law).

After making one quick examination of me, Dr. Curran diagnosed me with a fracture in the back of my skull and a serious concussion in the front. My parents came up to Worcester and drove me to St. Elizabeth's Hospital in Brighton, where I was treated under the care of Dr. Thomas F. Broderick, Sr., a surgeon in Boston. After taking a lumbar puncture of me, Dr. Broderick confirmed Dr. Curran's diagnosis.

I spent the next several weeks in the hospital and three months after that at home recuperating. I returned to school a few days before finals—on which I did sufficiently well to graduate from Holy Cross on June 12, 1940, although my time away from school lowered my cumulative average from 85% to 84%. I missed the Dean's List by one percentage point, after having been on it consecutively for three and a half years.

However, with the good sales record I had selling Fuller Brushes, I felt that I was assured the full-time job with Burroughs Adding Machine in Boston that Roy Scott, the Boston manager in 1939, had promised me. When I went in to see Mr.Scott after graduation, he was no longer there, having been replaced by a Mr. Frank Luby, who knew nothing about any arrangement and told me they only hired people with an M.B.A. degree and an average age of 24.

After I showed him my Fuller Brush record and my results in selling in college, he hired me on a probationary basis. I did quite well with Burroughs during the two years I spent with them.

CHAPTER EIGHT

COMBAT DUTY (1943-1945)

On December 7, 1941, all America was shocked by the news of the Japanese attack on Pearl Harbor. Within twenty-four hours after the attack, President Roosevelt and Congress announced that a state of war existed between the United States of America and the Japanese and German forces.

Unlike the days of the Korean and the Vietnam conflicts, all America seemed to rise to the occasion, and most every able-bodied American—men and women—wanted to volunteer for service. My sons, I believe, will never understand my actions at the time.

I had been drafted back in June 1940 for service in the Army. After taking my physical at the Commonwealth Armory on Commonwealth Avenue in Brighton, the eye doctors told me I had 20/2000 vision, which meant that what a person with normal eyesight could see at 2,000 feet, I could see only at 20 feet. The draft board told me that not only I would be classified 4-F, but also, in its opinion I would never be able to serve in the Armed Forces.

I returned to my job as a salesman for Burroughs and watched as all my buddies at work or at home signed up or were drafted for military service. Someone told me I could serve my country by becoming an air raid warden. After a not-too-vigorous training program, I was duly installed and became a Unit Chief of Air Raid Wardens (perhaps I was given this responsibility because most of the other Air Raid Wardens were 50, 60, or 70 years old, and many of them were not in too good shape).

We had nightly drills and once a week ran a mock air raid, where it was our job to roam the streets in our area with flashlights that were covered by a black cloth with only a pinhole for light. Our job was to canvass the neighborhood and reprimand any home where we found there were lights showing.

For the next eighteen months, I tried and tried to join the military—from the Navy, to the

Coast Guard, to the ground crew of the Air Force, to the Marines, and even to the Army. Once they heard I was 4-F and tested my eyes, they all threw up their hands in disgust and said I should never be accepted in any branch of the service.

Finally, one of my older friends, who was not in the draft, gave me a suggestion. He said, "If you really want to join up, take my advice and go down to New York City to the recruiting station down on Whitehall Street" (near Wall Street).

By now, it was May 15th (what I used to think was my birthday, which turned out to be incorrect as I have related above). The recruiting station was a madhouse that Fifteenth Day of May in 1942. Literally hundreds and yes, even thousands, of American youths were jamming the doors to get in and enlist in the service. With that bedlam, it was easy to suggest to the corporal taking the eye exams that I take the eye test with my glasses on first and then without them (without changing the chart). I said, "E," and he said, "You're in."

A bunch of us enlistees were loaded up in big two-and-a-half-ton Army trucks and brought out to Camp Upton (out on Long Island where Irving Berlin had written his famous war songs in World War I). We spent the day getting all kinds of shots, getting Army clothes (some that fit and some that didn't), and ending the long day by taking the Army General IQ Tests and the Army's Mechanical Aptitude Test. I was fortunate enough (with my Boston Latin School and Holy Cross education) to do quite well on both tests, with a 152 on the General Aptitude Test and a 148 on the Mechanical Aptitude Test.

The next day, we received our orders on where we would take our basic training course of 13 weeks. All of us who received 135 or more on the General Aptitude Test (plus some entertainers, good athletes, and people with strong political ties) were ticketed for assignment to the Army Air Force Base at Mitchell Field in Garden City, Long Island.

I was placed in the Air Force Intelligence Department. My first days in the Air Force were easy, dull, and frustrating. After four weeks in the service, I noticed an announcement on the bulletin board asking for volunteers for the post baseball team. Figuring it might be more interesting than what I was doing and not expecting to be selected, I signed up along with about

100 others who felt it might be "nice easy duty." After a couple of weeks of practice, I was amazed to see I had made the team, with a squad of 25 out of the original 100. It was a most pleasant summer of 1942: Every day on which we had a scheduled game, we would be excused early (usually in mid-afternoon) so we could load up in an Army truck for our trip across Long Island to play a team such as Grumman Aircraft, Republic Steel, or Fort Dix.

After the games, the opposing team would treat us to a steak and beer "blast," and we would return to Mitchell Field. The season ended in September, and then duty became most dull again.

I had been promoted from private to private first class and received a raise from $21 to $28 a month, so I decided to apply for admission to Officers Candidate School. After several interviews, I was accepted at Chemical Warfare Officers Training School in Edgewood Arsenal, Maryland, for the next class, which began in mid-December.

Going through Officers Candidate School—especially in Edgewood, Maryland, from mid-December to March—was no "apple pie." We received more true basic training in those three months than we did the first seven months at Mitchell Field (where we never went though an obstacle course or even fired a rifle). In early March, I was one of those who had survived and received my orders to Camp Sibert, Alabama (near Birmingham).

That two months' duty was quite interesting. I was given an assignment as a junior officer in a "smoke pot" platoon of all Afro-American soldiers. A "smoke pot" platoon was responsible for spreading smoke over an area to camouflage the troops.

In May, I received my orders to depart for overseas duty to some destination—unknown to all of us, although all kinds of rumors were floating around camp. It was only after five days at sea that we were notified of our final destination: Oran in North Africa.

After a very rough voyage down in the hold of the ship, we landed in Africa and were assigned to a replacement depot in Mezz-El-Kabir. We spent a few weeks there and then received our permanent orders to join the US 3rd Division in North Africa. We fought through Sicily during July and August and landed in Italy in September. We were then transferred into the

French Army, giving its infantry support with our 4.2 Mortar Battalion. The fall of 1943 saw us working our way against strong enemy opposition, as we headed for the Monte Cassino area. The weather was cold and damp—first rain (sometimes torrential) and then, in late fall, heavy snowstorms. I remember spending Thanksgiving of 1943 in a little town called Filignano in Italy and, between mortar and artillery barrages from the enemy, eating a semi-warm Thanksgiving turkey, which our company's kitchen crew cooked under most trying circumstances.

From Thanksgiving 1943 until June 1944, my 3rd Chemical Mortar Battalion was attached to the Free French Army as a support arm in their tedious, slow movement to Rome. I was then a second lieutenant and platoon leader. Each platoon had six squads (mortar gun crews) and two officers, one staff sergeant, and four sergeants. My job as a platoon leader was to give aid and encouragement and direction to my platoon.

Every few nights, one of us officers would sign up a reconnaissance squad to cross over to the enemy lines and find out what the Germans were doing. Ironically, the Germans would be sending their own recon squads over to our lines to see that we were doing. It was dangerous duty, and we were told by our company commander, a Captain John Moore (of Baton Rouge, Louisiana) that if one of our recon squad was missing, our strict orders were to abandon him and make sure the balance of the squad arrived back in friendly lines safely and without further mishap. It was a tough decision to have to make, but as we became more experienced in combat and recon squad adventures, we could see why this stand was necessary.

We made advances and had withdrawals as we edged ever so slowly from one hill to another valley to another hill towards Rome. In late December, we had an unfortunate experience when the first of several premature barrel explosions (because of defective mortar fuses) killed four members of our mortar gun crew.

The 4.2 Mortar was originally designed by the United States Army to be ready to bombard the enemy with chemical gases—if they started "chemical warfare," as the Germans did in World War I. Thank God, we experienced no chemical warfare for the entire war. Since we were not going to have to use these 4.2 Mortars for deadly gases, they acted as a support group for the US

Infantry and for the Free French Army under General Charles de Gaulle. The effectiveness of the 4.2 Mortar became apparent quite early in the Italian Campaign. It was one of the few weapons the Allied Forces had that could be used when the enemy was between 300 and 1,000 yards from our troops. With all the hills and mountains ahead of us between Naples and Rome, the trajectory of the 4.2 Mortar (a trajectory similar to the flight of a nine iron or wedge in today's game of golf) was most useful.

The German Army's famous 88s could not reach us if we had our gun positions in the opposite side of the mountain from the *enfilade* (a target vulnerable to sweeping gunfire from the enemy). But, then, the German Army came up with their *Nebelwerfers*—the horrifying "screaming meemies" mortars. They had the same effect as our 4.2's, plus they had a terrifying "scream" as they came down on top of us. As long as you were inside the umbrella (in the middle of the mortar shells flying down upon you), you were all right, but they wreaked havoc on the ones in the outside of the umbrella.

My job as a platoon leader, in addition to my semi-weekly leading a recon squad, was to supervise my gun crews and/or to act as a forward observer. Being a forward observer meant that my radio operator (who carried his radio on his back tuned in to the gun position) and I would be given by the company commander or the battalion commander a target that we should aim our mortars at in order to inflict heavy casualties on the enemy. I would take my little map, which covered about one square mile or less of territory. The map was covered by plastic and showed the gun position, the enemy target, and the location of my forward observation post. Obviously, in order to see the target with the naked eye, we would have to move forward, usually to a high point where visibility would be direct and clear. In many cases, we would be quite a distance ahead of the mortar gun crews and ahead of the infantry we were supporting.

You must realize that the enlisted men in the Free French Army were French colonials, who did not speak French, but Arabic. The junior officers and the non-commissioned officers were French and spoke that language well, but spoke very little English. My weak French (five years of French in high school and college) was not too helpful, because there are so many French dialects (patois), and military French is so different from academic French.

The colonials were not too happy with the Free French and had a bad habit of stealing everything they could get their hands on—including your watch if you were not too careful. The French officers and noncoms were most emotional, and I witnessed young French officers, dying from a direct mortar hit, crying out as they died, "Viva La France!"

Christmas of 1943 was spent in the mountains surrounding Monte Cassino, on a mountain called Mount Cairo. It was cold, nasty, and blowing hard for three or four days before and after Christmas Day. The nice thing about Christmas was receiving much mail and gifts from the States. Mail call was about nine o'clock at night, when the Mule Trains came to the upper side of the mountain where we were dug into foxholes waiting for the next call for more firepower of the mortars of for another of those deadly recon patrols. At or about nine o'clock (depending upon the good fortune of the mule drivers to escape injury or death, as the enemy kept up their mortar barrages night and day), the mule trains arrived. The most important cargo the mules brought to us was more ammunition (mortar shells) and warm clothes, especially warm socks and new combat boots, as "trench feet" was rampant. Some of the more serious cases developed gangrene, and some even had to have their feet amputated.

The mail and packages came last, once the essential ammo and clothes were loaded on the mules. The French goumieres (colonial troops) had the hideous job of literally dragging these stubborn mules up the hills to our front line positions. We could hear the mules (as well as the colonial troops) screaming and hollering as mortar shells would come pouring in from the enemy lines. We had many casualties—human and mule—and many times it would take the mule caravans anywhere from one to three hours for an ascent that would take us today not more than 20 or 30 minutes.

On January 12, 1944, my radio operator and I were up at a forward observation post (about 1,000 yards from the gun position) when we noticed three German fighter-bomber planes coming toward us from enemy positions. As they neared us up on the high ground, they seemed prepared to strafe us, but the Lord was with us. They passed over us, but then dropped three bombs over our battalion position, one hitting our battalion headquarters, one the French Army's battalion headquarters, and the third landing directly on a big US Army truck loaded down with German prisoners. My radio operator and I hustled back to battalion headquarters and found out we had lost our entire headquarters staff—including the battalion commander, our battalion supply officer, and several other officers and men. Within two minutes, our battalion was depleted, and every officer and noncom moved up in rank on a temporary basis. Our whole outfit was ordered back to division headquarters to be brought back up to normal strength by calling up replacement officers and men from the nearest replacement depots.

We had to refortify our outfit many other times during the balance of World War II until, in the last days of the war, we were sent older men (some over 40), young 17 year olds, and some not in too good shape for combat. For example, late in the war, one of my capable sergeants, who had already had over 500 days of combat, was accidentally killed by a "raw recruit" who had never been taught how to clean his rifle safely. I was standing right next to my sergeant, and the bullet whizzed by me and hit him square in the forehead. I had to pull some of my veteran troops off the recruit.

We were tied up right across from Mount Cassino for months on end and "survived" day by day with the same old rituals: recon patrols, instructions to fire on enemy targets, and more and more casualties—some serious, some deadly, and some of a minor nature.

As our log of days on the line passed the two, three, four, and five hundred mark, we did get, every three or four weeks, a day or two of furlough to places like Sorrento or the Isle of Capri. It was a real tonic for us, even though we realized only too well what was in store for us when we returned to the front. Some of our officers and troops told me the same after returning from 45-day leaves in the States. Finally, the big day came, and on May 11, 1944, we readied to push out of Cassino and bypass the enemy instead of attacking it head on. After a tremendous artillery and air force barrage from the Allied forces, we kicked off at 0800 hours; our objective was the capture of Rome. It took us from May 11th to June 5th— a period of 25 days—to accomplish our objective.

Before we reached Rome, it had been declared an "open city" by the retreating Germans. However, even as we roared down the highways in jeeps, tanks, and trucks; even as we entered the glorious city of Rome, with the Italians greeting us with flowers, kisses, and cheers, every once in a while a German sniper would take a shot at us from a fourth- or fifth-floor apartment window, and we would have to send a squad of Americans up to flush the German out of his hiding.

In spite of the frequent interruptions by sniper fire, it was a historic and colorful event as we roared into the Eternal City. Our appreciation of it was dulled temporarily when we received orders from Division headquarters that we would not stop in Rome, but continue to pursue the departing Germans north of the city. After meeting sporadic resistance, we reached the city of Viterbo (about 90 miles north of Rome), where we had orders to temporarily halt our march. (When I say that the resistance from the German Army was light and sporadic, I don't mean that we suffered no casualties, but I am merely quoting John Ellis: "Compared to other invasions, the resistance was light INITIALLY.") Three or four days later, a few of us officers and men were given a two-day pass to visit Rome.

By the this time, the rear echelon of high-ranking officers and troops from the Quartermasters Corps, Military Police, and other branches of support had arrived in Rome and quartered themselves down for a long stay.

Five or six of my troops and I had the wonderful opportunity to have a semi-private audience with His Holiness Pope Pius XII. Our semiprivate audience was much smaller than the ones held today with only 40 or 50 Army troops in attendance.

Our release of Rome and its excitement were lessened by the fact that one day after our capture of Rome, the big D-Day Invasion of the Normandy Beachhead occurred. Since the invasion of northern France had been in the works for months and months, it immediately took away the "glamour" of our capture of Rome.

We settled in the Viterbo area for the next few weeks until we were given orders to head south to the Italian town of Pozzuoli for amphibious training on the beaches of southern Italy. Here again all details were cloaked in secrecy, but we all had our "guesses" of our destination. Then, on August 14, 1944, we loaded onto troop ships and formed the biggest armada ever seen on the Mediterranean Sea.

Before we leave the Italian Campaign, I would suggest to all who read these memoirs to look up in your library the book entitled *Cassino: The Hollow Victory* by John Ellis (McGraw-Hill, 1984). The author is an American soldier who spent approximately 300 days at the front in the Cassino campaign. I can assure you that John Ellis has caught the flavor of the suffering, the rain, the mud, the snow, and the mountains better than anyone I know. It was certainly a "hollow victory," and I agree that many mistakes were made by the generals of the American, British, Canadian and other forces.

John Ellis seems to feel that the High Command of the Free French Army made many fewer tactical mistakes than all the other Allied commanders. This is a subjective opinion, but one with which I agree, having been attached to both the French Army and to the American army over that span of time. John Ellis writes, "The terrain is virtually impassable; a long spine of steep mountains with narrow littorals and rivers draining from the spine—a formidable natural area on which the Germans had skillfully improved. Wherever Allied forces tried to climb, the Germans had perfect cover and observatory positions." You will find the book most interesting reading.

At Pozzuoli, we had more retraining and dry runs for the invasion of southern France. Day after day, we practiced and practiced—not without unforeseen casualties. When the landing barges were not brought near enough to shore, some GI's (with heavy field packs) would sink into water about six or seven feet deep and go to the bottom with a thud—never to be seen again. It was work, work all day and usually tactics training at night—with a few nights to check the city of Naples. Much Italian wine was consumed and much cognac, since many of the soldiers felt they more than likely would never survive the D-Day landings.

On August 14th, the night before D-Day, Winston Churchill, safely ensconced in the flagship of the British navy, gave a most inspiring speech in his inimitable fashion over the loudspeaker system of the huge armada to all of the Allied troops. I paraphrase: *Men, tomorrow you will be a part of the greatest armada the Mediterranean Sea has even seen, and you will be a part of the beginning of the final push to Berlin.* The tremendous invasion force landed at H-Hour—0800 hours, preceded the night before by courageous paratroopers, demolition experts, and other necessary troops.

That night, after moving almost 20 miles inland into the town of Saint-Tropez, we bivouacked for the night. Much as we tried to impress upon our troops to "dig in," because the German forces, both land and air, would be most apt to counterattack, many of our troops "disappeared" to find the "wine, women, and song" of this beautiful little town, which had been before (and is now) a lovely summer town like some of our towns on Cape Cod.

While we were at Pozzuoli, I received three medals: General Juin of the Free French Army presented me with the prestigious Croix de Guerre Medal—a medal certainly not well-deserved, but in any case a great thrill to me—for action during the Cassino campaign. The other two medals were the American Army's Purple Heart Medal for injuries suffered in combat (I sustained shrapnel wounds in my leg, where shrapnel fragments remain today) and the Bronze Star for bravery in combat on May 14, 1944, as we kicked off from Cassino on the way to Rome. I still have the citation for the Bronze Star and for the Croix de Guerre and the actual Purple Heart and the Croix de Guerre medals.

After a few days fighting around Saint-Tropez, we started to move north, helping in the capture of the French cities of Marseilles and Toulon. Then, suddenly, we were given orders from higher headquarters to participate in "Project Bibo," a code name for a campaign to travel northeast over 100 miles behind the German lines and turn back into Italy towards Turin to cut off the entire German Army still in Italy.

Night after night, under cover of darkness, we rode in jeeps, tanks, and trucks into the Maritime Alps to reach the small town of Briancon, within two miles of the Italian border. When we bivouacked for the night, all was calm and quiet. However, at dawn the next day, all "Hell" broke loose, as, unknown to us, the German Army had come down from Italy and taken positions high up in the mountain, completely surrounding us. They had all their artillery and mortars keyed in on us, and we were practically annihilated. We had 6,000 French and American troops in our task force at the beginning, and when we finally escaped from the noose the Germans had around us, we had a scant 600 troops left. Not all our troops were killed or taken prisoner; some of the French troops just changed into farmer's garb and went back to tilling the fields. All I remember is that Colonel Bibo gave me strict orders to hold a bridge coming out of Briancon and he would return. Unfortunately, unlike General MacArthur, he never did return.

We finally fought our way out of the pincers and arrived back in the beautiful city of Grenoble. Obviously, with the beating we had taken, we had to be withdrawn from the front lines for a few days to be restructured and replaced with new troops.

After the task force Bibo fiasco, we headed into the Vosges Mountains and went back on the front lines. Fierce fighting ensued for the next few months, at which time we were ordered to the rear, near Wissemburg, Germany.

We all felt relieved that we would be off the front lines for Christmas. All plans were changed a few days later, when Battalion ordered us to gather up all our troops and prepare to take the long ride on jeeps, tanks, and trucks to a town in Belgium called Arlon (which we later found out was only 30 miles from another town, little known to us at that time, named Bastogne, Belgium).

People in the States undoubtedly knew far more about what was going on in the Battle of the Bulge than we did, but we quickly learned. Our job was to head for Bastogne and try to help rescue some of our troops that were surrounded in that town. At that time, we were detached from the Free French Army and assigned to the American 4th Division (an armored division; we acted as mortar support for them). We fought our way through dense woods with snow three or four feet high in drifts and bad weather which prevented our Air Force from flying most important sorties. Many of our men came down with pneumonia, and others developed trench feet. We still had to check ID's, because some Germans in the area were dressed in American Army uniforms and could speak perfect English. We even tried to find out if they were Americans by asking who had won the World Series in 1942 (St. Louis Cardinals vs. NY Yankees), but that did not always work.

Finally, good weather dawned, and our Air Force hit the skies once more. With that impetus and the bravery of our troops, we finally cut through into Bastogne and rescued the Allied forces that were still there. At the end of the Battle of the Bulge, we were sent back to the rear to heal our wounded and, once more, to be replenished with replacement troops, and then we were off for Germany.   From Bastogne, we headed northeast towards Hanover, Germany, where we crossed the Rhine and proceeded on to Berlin. However, since I was the last officer left in the battalion who had not been given a 45-day leave in the USA, I was given orders to go back to the States. I received this news with mixed feelings, as I remember how many of our officers who had gone home for a 45-day leave dreaded the thought of returning to the front lines, as they suspected they would get wounded or killed in the days ahead.

By this time it was early April 1945; most of us felt that the war in Germany would be over before we returned, and, thus, the chances of being wounded or killed were slight unless you had a jeep accident or stepped on a land mine. It took a few weeks to reach LeHavre, France, our port of debarkation for the States. In fact, we arrived in LeHavre to hear the news of President Roosevelt's death in Warm Springs, Georgia, and had a most impressive retreat service for him at our port of debarkation. A few days later, we loaded on to the "luxurious" Liberty Ships, where six officers and/or men occupied a space six feet long and seven feet high down in the bilge of the ship. It was no picnic going home, as many of the troops were dreadfully seasick and threw up all over the sleeping quarters. It was on the ship that we heard rumors, and then the true facts of the end of the War in Europe.

It was on V-E Day, May 8, 1945, that we landed in the "Good Old US of A." After landing in the Brooklyn Navy Yard, we were sent by military train to the Army camp nearest to our home, which in my case was Fort Devens, Ayer, Massachusetts (closed by Congress in 1996).

My brother, Tom, and his two-year-old son, "Butch," met me at the camp, and we left for a monstrous welcome home party at my house in Brighton. People kept coming and going all day long and well into the night. My mother thought I was now completely safe, but didn't realize that, although most of the enlisted men would be promptly discharged under the military system of points earned because of medals, time served overseas, and in combat, the officers were "invited" to stay in the service until the Japanese war ended.

After a 30-day leave at home, I received my orders to Camp Butner, North Carolina, where I was to be retrained for duty in Japan. I returned home from Germany at 165 pounds, but after two or three months on home leave and waiting around at Camp Butner for further orders, I was back up to 200 pounds. At Camp Butner, we just sat around, attended training classes, ate too much, and learned something about Japan and its soldiers.

After V-J Day (the end of the war in Japan, August 15, 1945), I was reclassified for limited duty because the shrapnel in my leg was kicking up again, causing phlebitis in my leg. I was sent to the Murphy General Hospital in Waltham for consultation between Army doctors as to whether or not it was advisable to remove the shrapnel.

On my own, I went to see Dr. Thomas Broderick Sr., a capable orthopedic surgeon in Boston. After thoroughly examining me, he advised me to forget the operation, because he felt it would cause a stiffness in my leg the rest of my life.

I finally received my orders to be honorably discharged from the Army as a captain in the Chemical Warfare Branch of the Army. With all the accumulated leave I had built up over months in combat, I was discharged on September 30, 1945, with the actual effective date being December 31, 1945. Looking back over the 50 years since I was in the Army, I realize all too well how good the Lord was to me in keeping me safe after over 700 days in combat.

I know now how strong and effective were the prayers of my mother and all the other friends of mine who prayed so much for me. There's an old expression: "Only the good die young," and perhaps there is something to it. In any case, my Faith leads me to believe that God had something in mind for me, and I hope I have paid God back in a small way for all He has done for me.

In the minds of the thousands of men and women who eagerly volunteered for active duty in World War II, it was a "justifiable war." The experiences of the Korean and the Vietnam conflicts make you wonder if any war is really "justifiable." Only God knows the answers, and I sincerely hope that we who fought in wars will be pardoned by the Good Lord for any sins we may have committed in waging war against the so-called "Enemy."

Let us all pray that this is the last war that any people will have to endure in the years ahead. No one wins in war, and very few benefit from any action they saw. The only benefit that some soldiers may have obtained from war is that, after seeing and experiencing the horrors of war, there should be very little that can cast fear into their hearts in civilian life. It is interesting that at the few 3rd Chemical Warfare Mortar Battalion reunions that we have attended, most of the stories are the humorous ones and not the tragic ones of the mud, blood, and suffering we all witnessed. Perhaps for the well-being and peace of mind of all of us, it is just as well I did see some tremendous acts of bravery by my comrades-in-arms and some terrible suffering by those who were wounded and killed.

After my return home from the war, I found out that my father wanted to sell the five cottages he had owned for years and rented out to summer people. I told him I would be interested, and he was quite surprised as he did not know that I had saved all my pay for two and a half years in the Army. I took out a mortgage to pay the balance, and had a sixth cottage built by Brooks Skinner Company of Quincy. It was a prefabricated cottage, and they built it in three days.

For the next eight to ten years, I rented five of the six cottages. The reason I rented only five out of six was that I let my father and mother (who were then almost 80 and 61 years of age, respectively) spend the summer in one cottage.

In the early 1950s, my July rentals approached me about the possibility of selling the cottages to them. Bill and Agnes Dowling bought one, Bud and Helen Ryan another, Dick and Terry Myles one. Bud Riley bought one, and the Myles later bought the Rileys' cottage for rental purposes. The fifth buyer was Mike Grealy, a field underwriter for Home Life, who bought it from Bud Ryan and Dick Myles for his cousins. The buyers of my cottages all have increased the value of my home because they invested several thousands of dollars to improve each one of them. In addition, and more importantly, the six families have been neighbors and good friends for an average of 60 years.

One year, in late August, Bud Ryan and I saw a young man bringing his cat boat ashore and loading it up on a trailer. We went down to talk to him, and he told us he was interested in selling it, as he would not be able to return to Brewster the following summer. Upon our asking the price for the boat, he mentioned 100 dollars would be sufficient. Bud and I conferred for a couple of moments and then decided to buy it jointly. The following spring, we worked long and hard in sanding down the bottom and in repainting the wooden boat.   Finally, we were ready to take our maiden voyage. Bud, Helen, Marion, and I boarded the sailboat, and I was appointed to take the tiller, as I had studied a book on how to sail. What a mistake. After a pleasant sail out from the beach, Marion decided she had had enough and wanted to go back to shore. When I told her I hadn't reached that section of the book as yet, I thought Marion was going to divorce me. However, with Bud's help, we managed to tack and arrive safely back to shore. That sail was Marion's last.

The summer was a catastrophe. Our sons thought that they weren't getting equal time, and the Ryan girls thought they were being cheated out of their time. Finally, Bud and I had had enough and, when he asked me to sell my half to him for $50, I agreed quickly and took Marion out to dinner with the proceeds. She was delighted.

CHAPTER NINE

BUILDING A CAREER

While I was on limited duty in the Army in the fall of 1945, I was having some serious thoughts about a possible career change, even though I had kept in touch with the people at Burroughs Adding Machine during the war. I received an interesting phone call from a man named "Chuck" Murphy, leaving word with my mother that he would like to talk to me about a possible career in the life insurance business. Frankly, I was not at all interested in the life insurance business at that time, but my mother suggested to me that I should at least return his call, as he was a fellow alumnus from Holy Cross College—having graduated 12 years before me. When I returned his call to tell him very politely that I wasn't interested in a career in the life insurance business, he said that was fine, but that he had heard of my Army career and would like to take me to lunch. At lunch, he suggested to me, as I had plenty of time and did not have to get back to the Murphy General Hospital right away, that I return with him to his office at 31 Milk Street in Boston and take an aptitude test that might tell me which career path I should be considering. Having nothing better to do, I complied with his wishes and took the series of tests. A few days later, "Chuck" called me back to tell me I had scored very highly on the test, and he would like to discuss it with me.

Over the next several weeks, I had several interviews with "Chuck" about a possible career in the life insurance business. I was faintly interested at first in building a clientele through "planned estates," and then became quite excited about it. When I went in to see the people at Burroughs and told them of such an opportunity, they laughed in my face and intimated that everyone in the life insurance business was either a crook or a failure.

The more they criticized the life insurance business, the more I wanted to investigate it further. In order to get a more objective opinion of the business, I went to see ten of my father's business associates in whom he had confidence. Nine of them said I would not be good in that field, and only one said, "You're just the man for it." The final decision was up to me, and I did a lot of soul-searching and praying as to my right choice. When I had finally decided to join Home Life with "Chuck" Murphy, I made an appointment to see him. Was I surprised. After I told him I had decided to join Home Life, he told me that Home Life did not want to hire me, because I was single and had very few potential clients in Boston who had incomes over $10,000 a year. He then told me that he had complete confidence in me, and that he was going to call the home office and tell them that he had already hired me (at $250 a month). He went on to say that, if the home office overruled him, he would tell them he would have the entire Holy Cross Alumni Association in Boston after him.

On November 19, 1945, I started with the Home Life in Boston as a fledging field underwriter. At the same time I started, there was an older, more mature, married man with children who began his career with the Home Life. After three months, I hadn't sold a penny, and he had sold over $100,000 of life insurance. Was I surprised when he came in to tell me that he had just resigned. When I asked him why, he said, "I may have sold $100,000 more than you; but I haven't received a single prestige recommendation, and you have over 50. I have nowhere to go, and you have lots of people to see." He was right, as in my fourth month, I finally started to see results and averaged over $70,000 of business a month over the next nine months—finishing the year with over $600,000 sold and ranking number eight in the entire company.

After 18 months as a salesman, I was given an opportunity to start in the management program with Home Life, as I had already recommended several men to Home Life (including my college classmate Joe Aieta, who has spent his entire career with Home Life and is still working for them on a reduced basis).

I was working five to six days a week and many nights when the GREATEST DAY of my life occurred on August 8, 1945. I had been spending my weekends at my beloved Brewster, and on that weekend, my mother mentioned there was a nice young lady named Marion spending some time that week with her mother at Tip-Top House (now, in 1996, called Beechcroft Inn) on Main Street in Brewster. I had met her the previous fall through my college classmate Joe Flynn at a

Holy Cross football game and had attended her father's wake in Needham the previous February. I went up to see her, and we went to a place called "Casa Madrid" over in South Yarmouth that night. We had a wonderful time dancing outdoors to one of the big bands of the era.   After two or three hours with her, I felt she was for me—but she doesn't quite remember it that way. In fact, she still insists that she never told me, "I would never marry you." In any event, 46 days later, I presented her in St. Joseph's Chapel at Holy Cross with an engagement ring. She recalls it was after a Holy Cross-Dartmouth Football Game. She agreed on the promise that we wouldn't get married until after the first anniversary of her father's death.

In those days, the Catholic Church would not allow weddings during Lent, so we decided on Easter Monday (the day after Easter), March 29, 1948, for our wedding day. On March 29, 1996, we celebrated the 48th anniversary of our wedding. Was I fortunate to have met and married such a wonderful woman, understanding and patient with me. She had to put up with all my shortcomings and has been a wonderful wife and mother.

One story that illustrates my shortcomings is of a day a heavy blizzard was forecast. I stayed in my office long after everyone else had left, and by the time I did finally leave, we were in the midst of a howling "white-out." I drove out Commonwealth Avenue to Brookline Avenue, and the snow was drifting three and four feet all around me. When I reached Brookline Village, it was hopeless; and I had to come to a complete stop. A short time later, the State Police came to my car and told me I would have to stay the night at the Brookline Fire Station. In the meantime, unbeknownst to me, my poor wife called my brother and her own brother to ask them to try to find me by retracing the path I would have taken from the office. After an hour or so of seeking, they found my car on Route 9 right near Brookline Village, but no sign of me. They returned to my house to tell my wife the news, and she had to await my arrival home after daylight the next day. Such is the life of a faithful wife.

CHAPTER TEN

MARRIED LIFE

As the MAGIC DAY of March 29, 1948, approached, both of us were helping (in a small way) Mrs. Riley (Marion's mother) with plans for the wedding. Even though she had become a widow in the past year, she handled the wedding arrangements with some help from Marion. Marion chose Ginny Flynn, her roommate at college, to be her maid of honor, and I selected my brother, Tom, to be best man. Marion's brother, George, was invited to give his sister away (in the absence of her father). My ushers were Bud Ryan, Bud Daley, Bill Dowling, Herb Minkel, Joe Flynn, and Dick Myles, while Marion selected for her bridesmaids Peggy Rogers, Rosamond Sheehan, Peggy Pat Hurley, and Joan Kalloch. The Wedding Mass, with the Rev. Fairbanks of St. Joseph's as Celebrant, was at the old St. Joseph's Church in Needham (long since torn down to be replaced on the same spot by the new St. Joseph's Church).

A scary (for me) occasion was when my friend from Burroughs, Bob Bennett, came to our house to pick up my parents to bring them to the wedding—leaving me dressed in tall hat and tails on the sidewalk outside my house (with no key to get back inside to make a call if necessary). It seemed like hours as I waited for my brother to come and pick me up for the wedding. Finally, he arrived, and we left Brighton and my home at 55 Wallingford Road for the last time. We had lived there 28 years.

It was a beautiful, warm day, and the wedding came off very smoothly. After the Mass, we headed first to Emmanuel College, where Marion, according to College tradition, visited the chapel at Emmanuel and received the prayers and best wishes of the Sisters of Notre Dame at Emmanuel.

There was another old tradition that all Emmanuel graduates and their new husbands would promise to say the Rosary every day of their married lives. I must confess we had every intention of carrying out this promise, and we did for a few years but, then, the arrival of five sons and our parental duties with them slowed down our promises. I hope the Lord will forgive us.

After our "way stop" at Emmanuel, we headed for the Woodland Country Club in Newton, where the reception was to take place. The wedding guests had been very patient with our detour at Emmanuel and had had plenty of time to visit the cocktail lounge at Woodland. After a most pleasant reception with an orchestra and dancing, we left for our honeymoon in our new 1948 Nash automobile. Marion tells me (although I am not sure if she is kidding or not) that after leaving the Woodland Country Club, we made a 180-degree turn and found ourselves back in front of the clubhouse again. Whether this a true story or not, we headed for New York City where I had, without Marion's knowledge, put a deposit down on a wedding night at the Waldorf-Astoria Hotel in Manhattan. All my well-laid plans almost went awry when, upon arriving at the Waldorf, I was politely but firmly told that they were completely sold out and had no room at the inn for us. I tried everything from praising them for their reputation to telling them that I thought they would keep a room for us as I had sent them the down payment of 35 dollars. Finally, after many conferences between the desk clerk and the night manager, they decided to give us the bridal suite—at the same price as would have been the cost of a regular room.

When we reached the suite, we found it to be magnificent and counted fourteen candles (lit by electricity) in the living room. The next night of our honeymoon, we went from the magnificence of the bridal suite at the Waldorf-Astoria to a strange, old-fashioned hotel in Dover, Delaware, with squeaky floors and spooky closets. It was fun in any case, and the next day we left for our final destination, the General Oglethorpe Inn on an island off the coast of Savannah, Georgia.

After a wonderful 12-day honeymoon, we made the return back to Boston and settled into a very nice new one-bedroom apartment at 81 Gerry Road (Hancock Village) in Chestnut Hill, Massachusetts.

The first year of married life was, I guess, typical, with several of our married friends (who had been married two or three years before us) visiting us with their new babies. I am afraid that Marion, after six months of married life and no babies, feared that she would never become pregnant.

On July 12, 1949, Marion presented me with our first baby—a boy with lots of hair on his head whom we named Paul Michael (who soon became P. Michael and then "Mike"). For a year and a half, life went on at 81 Gerry Road. I was still working three or four nights a week with the Home Life and Marion was surviving all the problems of new motherhood.   In the summer of 1950, we were given the opportunity of advancing in the management program of Home Life and entering the home office in New York, just after we had bought our first home—a six-room, brand new Cape on Stockdale Road in Needham. Luckily, through Bud Ryan, we were able to sublet it to a man named Ed Dobbyn and his wife. Ed was just entering a two-year program sponsored by the Navy at the Harvard Business School, and we felt, at the time, that it would mesh beautifully with my two-year stay in New York. So, on Labor Day weekend, we took off for Plainfield, New Jersey, where we would be quartered for the following two years at garden-type apartments owned by Home Life.

After trying to settle in on Labor Day weekend, I came home the day after Labor Day to give Marion the surprising (and not too happy) news that I would be leaving for Virginia the following day for a week's stay at a life insurance conference at Virginia Beach. And so, Marion's turbulent life began with one-and-a-half-year-old Mike, and then finding out that she was once again pregnant. This was another of the crosses Marion had to bear with me, as I was on the road seven months out of the next eight. We thought our second child was going to be born at the Muhlenberg Hospital in Plainfield in September 1951, but, thanks be to God, we were notified in April of 1951 that I was to be appointed as an agency manager for Home Life in Boston (a second agency) immediately.

CHAPTER ELEVEN

FIVE SONS

Our early days of marriage were never dull. For the first three months as an agency manager, I was trying to build an agency from "scratch" in Boston. Marion had to remain in Plainfield, while I lived at the Parker House in Boston. Finally, when I rented another apartment back in Hancock Village at 220 Gerry Road (as we couldn't evict our good tenants, the Dobbyns, until September 1952), Marion and Mike joined me just a few months before Bill was born at the Saint Elizabeth's Hospital in Brighton (the same hospital where Mike was born).

Finally, in September 1952, Ed Dobbyn graduated from Harvard Business School, and we were able to move back into our first home at 80 Stockdale in Needham. I was struggling trying to build an agency for Home Life while Marion had her own problems dealing with two small babies; Mike was two to three years old and Bill was in his first year of life.

In the fall of 1952, Marion found out that she was pregnant for the third time. With three children on the horizon, we decided we needed a larger house than the small two-bedroom we had on Stockdale Road. So, we looked and looked and finally found the ideal house for a growing family—at 19 Fair Oaks Park in Needham, a large, eight-room brick house close to schools, playgrounds, and church. With David's debut in June of 1953 (and he's been debuting every year since as an actor and director of plays on and off Broadway), we had three sons: Mike, aged four; Bill, aged two; and David, a small baby.

The next year, Mike started kindergarten at St. Joseph's school, but for the first year, because St. Joseph's School wasn't ready, he had to take a bus two miles to St. Bartholomew's School on the other side of Needham. Marion had an awful job—dropping Mike off at the school bus stop and then making sure he arrived home after the short half day of kindergarten. Obviously, she had to take the other two small children with her on the walk to the bus stop. For the next five years, our family size remained at five: three sons and Marion and I.

Then, on August 11, 1958, our fourth son came into the picture: John Paul Saint. By that time, Mike was nine years old and partially on his own; Bill was seven and David five. Time went by and we survived with a growing family.

Eight years later, our youngest son, Joseph Richard, arrived, born in the Glover Hospital in Needham. Mike was now 17 years old and a senior at Boston College High School getting ready to enter Holy Cross College a year and a half later; Bill was 15 years old and a sophomore at St. Sebastian's School, then in Newton; David was in his 13th year and getting ready to graduate from St. Joseph's School in Needham; while Jack was eight and in the grammar school at St. Joseph's. Joe's birth completed our family. Even though we would have liked to have had a daughter somewhere along the way, we were blessed with five healthy sons (and later on we had five granddaughters).

So finished our early years of marriage and births of our five sons. Over the following years our five sons each matured in his own way.

MIKE

Mike graduated from Holy Cross in 1971 as a Presidential Scholar with a major in political science. He seemed to like the newspaper business and started his career with the *Catholic Free Press* in Worcester, moving to the *Marlboro Enterprise*, and then the *Quincy Patriot Ledger*, first as a reporter covering local town news and then on to the State House as a State House reporter. At this point in his reportorial career, he applied for a position as a press agent at the State House. After several interviews, he found out that the position was Press Agent for Lieutenant Governor Thomas O'Neill, Jr., son of the then speaker of the House in Washington. Mike spent almost four years with Lieutenant Governor O' Neill and then formed his own public relations and communications business, called Saint Communications, first in Quincy and then in Hingham (where it is still located today, with another office in Nashville, Tennessee).

In 1984, Mike met and fell in love with Anne Boggess from Guntersville, Alabama. They were married on September 1, 1984, and now have two beautiful daughters, Mary Haden (Molly) Saint, age four and Sarah Riley Saint, age two. They have a new home in Franklin, Tennessee, and Mike commutes between his offices in Hingham, Massachusetts and Nashville, Tennessee.

BILL

Bill attended Holy Cross for a year and a half and then withdrew to attend St. John's Seminary in Brighton, as he felt he had a vocation for the Catholic priesthood. However, after a short stay of a few months, he decided it wasn't for him and left the Seminary to attend and graduate from Framingham State College in Framingham, Massachusetts. Bill spent ten years working with retarded people, a couple of years as an executive with the Boy Scouts, one year in the insurance business, and is currently a certified nurse's aide and working in a nursing home in Norwood. None of his jobs has been high-paying, but he certainly has done a lot for humanity. Bill is still single as of 1996.

DAVID

David has had the Theater in his blood since his early days in school, when he acted in all the school plays. At Boston College High School, he had the lead in many school productions and culminated his successful career in B.C. High School Dramatics by being named the Outstanding Actor and Director by the *Boston Globe* Awards Committee.

He was accepted to Holy Cross College in the fall of 1971 and spent many hours rehearsing for plays at Holy Cross. Early in his freshman year, he told his mother that he was spending four to five hours a day in rehearsing for school plays, and she warned him his marks might suffer. On his next semester report card, he had four 3.5's and one 4.0. From that time on, we never did worry about his marks, and he graduated one half of a point from being Summa Cum Laude.

After graduating from Holy Cross in 1975, he headed to New York to seek his fame and fortune on the New York stage. He studied under the famous Broadway actress Uta Hagen for three years and accepted parts in all kinds of productions. Some days, we would send him care packages, and he often lived on tuna fish and peanut-butter-and-jelly sandwiches. He took all kinds of part-time jobs to keep the "wolf" from his door, but he hung in there, and successes started to come to him.

After ten years in acting, David decided that his forte was in directing others, and he launched a career in direction. Here again, he had a tough row to hoe, but he had the determination and commitment to "hang in there." As of 1996, he is really starting to move. He has earned many awards for directing, and one play he has directed, Anne Meara's *After-Play*, is, as of this date, the longest-playing drama on or off Broadway, having just completed its fourteenth month. Jane Powell has just replaced Rita Moreno, and Anne Meara, the play's author, performs two parts in the show at different times.

In January of 1996, David kindly sent us round-trip plane tickets to Seattle, Washington, to see the successful play by Arthur Miller, *The Price,* which David directed.

In May 1996, David directed *on* Broadway a modern adaptation of Moliere's *Tartuffe*, with John Glover.

From June 1, 1996, to January 1,1997, David will be the new assistant artistic director at the prestigious Seattle Repertory Theater.

JACK

Jack graduated from Holy Cross in 1980, and though he majored in psychology, he took four electives in computer science—in which he had a 4.0 average. After graduation, he embarked on a successful career in software.

He just left one successful software company, which had gone from six people to 168 in six years and then was sold by the two principals for 40 million dollars.

Jack has formed his own company, called IDFM (Integrating Data For Management), with another fellow worker from Spectrum, the last company he was with, where he was a group manager. In 1983 Jack met, fell in love, and married Karen Ruggeiro from Natick. They now have three daughters: Amy, age nine; Michelle, age five; and Kaitlyn, age two; and have a lovely new home in Sudbury, Massachusetts, with four bedrooms, a swimming pool, and a cabana.

JOE

Joe graduated from Roxbury Latin School in 1984 as a National Merit Scholar and entered Holy Cross. After four years, he graduated with Honors and a Bachelor of Arts degree with a double major in classics and theater arts. After one year of working as a lighting designer in various theaters, Joe was awarded a three-year teaching fellowship at the School of Drama at University of Virginia. In June 1992, Joe graduated with a Master of Fine Arts with Honors and won the Best Student-Teacher Award from the University of Viginia. He then left for New York to qualify for his United Scenic Artists designation.

A year after Joe graduated from Holy Cross, he married his college sweetheart, Beth Cavallaro, from Naples, Florida. However, five years later, Beth had severe problems with depression and decided to split up with Joe and go out on her own in South Carolina. She was a lovely girl—intelligent, beautiful, and from a nice family—but unfortunately, the marriage did not work out and ended in divorce in 1993. After 40 weeks on and off Broadway, Joe received his U.S.A. designation and has had many lighting design positions since that time, some as the head lighting designer and some as the assistant lighting designer. Three of his plays have appeared on Broadway : *The Kiss of the Spider Woman*, Brian Friel's *Translations*, and in March 1996, the Royal Shakespearean Company's production *of A Midsummer Night's Dream.*

CHAPTER TWELVE

GRANDCHILDREN ARRIVE

After our five sons had graduated from college, we looked forward with anticipation to the birth of our grandchildren. Our first grandchild, a daughter to our fourth son, Jack, and his wife, Karen, was named Amy, and is now in the third grade at John Nixon Grammar School in Sudbury, Massachusetts. She, like our other four granddaughters, has been a blessing to us, and we have derived lots of satisfaction from her.

Our next grandchild, Michelle, was also born to Jack and Karen, on June 5, 1991; and she will be entering kindergarten in September of 1996.

Our third grandchild was born to our oldest son, Mike, and his wife, Anne. Her name is Mary Haden "Molly" Saint, and she is a real "doll." She loves to paint with her paternal grandmother and is attending preschool in Franklin, Tennessee. Now four years old, she is quick to learn, and calls us whenever she can.

Kaitlyn Saint, the third child of Jack and Karen, is our fourth grandchild, and was born in February 1994. At two years of age, she is walking and trying to talk as much as possible.

On March 29th, our 46th wedding anniversary, our most recent grandchild, Sarah Riley Saint, was born to Mike and Anne. She's a "holy terror" and tries to follow every move that her big sister Molly makes. She is very different from Molly, but they are both very cute and lovable. Here's hoping that the Good Lord blesses us with more grandchildren in the future, but one never knows and must pray for what is best for all concerned. Marion had no sisters and neither did I, and we had five sons and no daughters; but now, thank God, we have five wonderful granddaughters.

CHAPTER THIRTEEN

VOCATIONS AND AVOCATIONS OF PAUL AND MARION SAINT

Between 1948 and 1983, I was trying to earn a living for my family by being successful in the life insurance business. It was most difficult and time consuming to work up the ladder with Home Life. Many evenings I was out until ten or eleven o'clock on appointments. I was fortunate that I had such an understanding helpmate as my good wife, Marion. Not only did she have to put up with my long hours, but also especially, early in my career of trying to build an agency, she would sacrifice buying her clothes so that I could invest money back into the business.

In 1951, we opened our agency for the Home Life in Boston. It was tough going these first few years, as I made mistakes in hiring people and sometimes made errors of judgment in working with the field underwriters.

After about ten years of going two steps backward and one step forward, progress seemed to come. By 1961, our agency started to climb in the standings of the company, and from that time on, although we did have our ups and downs, we were usually in the top ten agencies of the company. From 1972 until my retirement as manager in 1983, we were usually second, third, or fourth in the company. Over the years, we were fortunate to win many agency awards in the company and were well-respected by the peers in my company and by the agency managers of other companies in the life insurance business. In the meantime, I received many professional designations, such as the Chartered Life Underwriters designation (C.L.U.), and the Chartered Financial Consultant Designation (ChFC). Both these designations required much serious study on my part, as the C.L.U. required 20 hours of examinations, while the ChFC required six examinations of two hours each.

I became quite active in the life insurance business, holding all offices of the C.L.U. chapter of Boston, and was chairman of the Managers Round Table, member of the Estate Planning Council, and a member the Boston Life Underwriters Association (from which I received in 1983 the Albert E. Richardson Award for Outstanding Contribution to the Life Insurance Industry). In Home Life, I became President of the Home Life Managers Association and was elected to the company's elite Hall of Fame in 1983.

Looking back at my long career in the life insurance business, I am very pleased with the business, my progress in it, and the income it gave my family. Just think, educating five sons through private elementary and high schools and private colleges was an investment of approximately $250,000 (after taxes), but Marion and I never regretted it. Don't think it was all "peaches and cream," because both Marion and I had to make supreme sacrifices to attain this level. Furthermore, I am certainly not so immodest to think that every decision I made in the business was the right one. Many times I would give a talk to life insurance managers in the United States and Canada. The title of my talk was, "How I Made 49 Percent Wrong Decisions BUT 51 Percent Right Decisions." My deep satisfaction was in the number of successful managers and field underwriters that I had the pleasure of recruiting into the business and helping in their progress.

While I was trying to build my lifetime career in the life insurance business, Marion was doing a marvelous job in her career of raising a family. It wasn't a "bed of roses" to bring up five sons, especially when the oldest was 17 when the youngest was born. Each of our sons, like most sons, was different, and Marion had to be a psychologist as well as nursemaid, cook, and baby-sitter to keep our sons in line. All of our sons had the typical childhood diseases and ran into the usual scrapes, but I personally feel that, because of Marion's understanding and patience, they all turned out well. We are both proud of all of them and love them dearly.

In the summers at Brewster, it was particularly tough for Marion because, in the early days of my working career, we had only one car, and she was on her own all week while I was working in Boston. Even when we advanced to two cars, it was tough—but tough to a different degree, as Mike had his license when Joe was just born, and many nights (as in most families) Marion had to worry (as most mothers do) when he was out too late. She had to follow our sons to Little League games (which she did when I couldn't), have Cub Scout Den Meetings at our house (for over a 17- year period). At one time, I honestly believe that at age 53 she was the oldest Den Mother in town.

Attending parents' meetings at school, seeing children in plays and concerts, and other parental duties required Marion to perform more service because of her husband's occupation. I, unlike many fathers who had nine-to-five jobs, would be working until ten or 11 at night, and she would cover for me.

In addition to being an excellent mother and wife, Marion still made the time to carry on with her interest in art and became president of the Needham Art Association. At that time of her life, she concentrated mostly oils, while in later life she centered more on watercolors. Marion was also most interested in our St. Joseph's Church, and worked as a volunteer at the Saint Joseph's School Library.

When we reached the Cape, and our sons were all on their own, Marion had time for even more avocations such as volunteering for over eight years to teach art (oils, watercolors, pastels, etc.) to senior citizens of Brewster at the Council on Aging. This avocation took three hours a week in class and often many additional hours at home thinking up projects and ideas for her students. She has spent, overall, more than 1,000 hours in this volunteer work.

She has been most active in the functions of Our Lady of the Cape Church as a Eucharistic Minister, as a volunteer bringing Communion to the elders at the Brewster Manor Nursing Home, vice president and program chairman of the Ladies Guild, volunteer at the Thrift Shop, facilitator of a group at Scripture Study, and other activities in the Church. Marion is also active in the Brewster Woman's Club, and she was publicity chairman for the Brewster Historical Society, and a member of the Brewster Garden Club.

I was also involved in many avocations. For example, I was extremely active in the Holy Cross Alumni affairs. I started out way back in 1940, immediately after graduation, when I was asked to be the sports editor of the *Crossbow*, monthly alumni newspaper for the Holy Cross Club of Boston. A year later I became the editor, advertising manager, and writer for the *Crossbow*. Before World War II, and immediately thereafter, I participated in the Holy Cross Club of Boston

Bowling League.

When I returned from the war, I reactivated my interest in Holy Cross affairs and became president of the Holy Cross Club of Boston, member of the General Alumni Association Board of Directors, and vice-chairman of the Holy Cross Associate Board of Trustees. Since 1949, I have been extremely active in all Holy Cross Alumni affairs and was awarded the "In Hoc Signo Award" in 1974 for outstanding service to the Holy Cross Alumni Association. From 1972 to 1974, I served as president of the Holy Cross General Alumni Association, traveling hundreds of miles across the country to visit Holy Cross Regional Clubs.

I was also active in town affairs. I was elected first to the Limited Town Meeting Form of Government of Needham as a Town Meeting member, and then was elected as a member and chair of the Needham Board of Selectmen where I served seven years, from 1963 until 1970. I was also chairman of the town of Needham's bicentennial celebration as well as vice president of the Needham Community Council and general chairman for Needham's United Fund Drive.

In the meantime, in 1953, I became a charter member of the new Needham Lions Club and served as its first full-time president, and as zone chairman, deputy district governor for three years. In 1960, I became district governor of District 33-K Lions, which covered 53 cities and towns from Framingham in the west to Bellingham in the southwest and Malden in the north. For outstanding service as a district governor, I was awarded the title of International Counselor of the Lions (the final district governor to be given that award).

In the meantime, I was president of the Needham Lions Club in 1954. In 1984, I was given the honorary title of a Melvin Jones Fellow and life membership in Lions International, and was selected as the Outstanding Lion in the Needham Lions Club. As far as activity in my church, St. Joseph's Catholic Church of Needham, I was an usher for 25 years, was general chairman of fund-raising for the Parish School, and was an active member of the St. Joseph's Saint Vincent de Paul Society.

I tried to stay close to our sons by coaching Little League for many years and served on the Boy Scouts Parents' Committee. I also coached St. Joseph's CYO Basketball program. When

Joe entered the Roxbury Latin School, Marion and I became chairpersons of the Parents Fund Drive.

I may have overlooked some programs that Marion and I were involved in, but as you can see, we were both most active in different avocations both in Needham and later on the Cape.

In addition, we have traveled extensively from 1973 to the present, visiting 13 foreign countries and 42 states.

CHAPTER FOURTEEN

PERMANENT MOVE TO BREWSTER

In 1983, I retired as manager of Home Life, but spent the next couple of years as director of management for Home Life and became a consultant and teacher of management for several companies. I had also been teaching at Northeastern University's School of Management since 1960 and continued that endeavor.

In 1986, Marion and I decided to make Brewster our permanent home. First, we bought a three-bedroom condo at Sea Pines Condominiums on Main Street in East Brewster, and we moved into that home for the first few winters. We lived in our summer home on Robbins Hill Road (Saint's Landing) from May until October. Finally, in 1993, we had it completely renovated. We increased the size and ended up with a four-bedroom, two-bath home. We had it fully insulated and changed our costly electric heat to oil heat, so that we were very comfortable even in the coldest winter nights.

In order to accommodate Marion's and my hobbies, we changed half of one bedroom into an art studio (with skylight) for Marion, and the other half into an office and computer room for me.

As we settled in to full-time life in Brewster, we continued many of the hobbies we had had in Needham. In addition to the activities mentioned in the previous chapter, Marion and I became very active in the Church's Scripture Study Group, each of us acting as facilitators.

We formed a card-playing group playing a funny game called "May I?", a derivative of contract rummy. Our next door neighbors, Bill and Agnes Dowling; one of my golfing partners, Bob Macklin, and his wife Barbara; and several widows from our area including Marguerite McGirr, Mary Carey, Gert Dillon, Margie Sullivan, and Marie Snyder were some of our weekly participants, and it was lots of fun.

I continued my activities with the Lions, joining the Dennis-Harwich Lions Club, and with town government. I transferred my membership from St. Joseph's Church in Needham to Our Lady of the Cape in Brewster and became a co-general chairman of the Church's fund-raising drive for a one-million-dollar new parish center. I also became a Eucharistic Minister, joined the Bible Group, was awarded the prestigious Marian Award by the bishop of Fall River,

I started, with the sanction of the pastor, a new Saint Vincent de Paul Society to help the needy with food, overdue rents, telephone, and electric bills. We now have ten members, five men and five women, who are caring for the needs of the less fortunate in the entire town of Brewster and the town of Dennis north of Route 6 (the Mid-Cape Highway).

In 1987, having been a permanent resident of Brewster—a town of 8,000 people in the winter and 35,000 in the summer—for only six months, I ran for and was elected Selectman of Brewster. As a selectman, I was also assessor, serving as chairman of the Board of Assessors for six years. I was also chairman of the Board of Selectmen for one year. I served on the Insurance Committee, was liaison to the library and the Golf Club Commission. I also was commissioner of Public Works, and carried out various other duties as selectman. After serving two full terms (six years) as a member of the Brewster Board of Selectmen, I announced my retirement from the Board (as I had always planned) in order to give others the opportunity to serve and bring in new ideas.

I continued to be active in Holy Cross Alumni affairs and was elected president of the Holy Cross Club of Cape Cod, program chairman, and was often acting secretary and chairman of many affairs on national levels. I was a member of the General Alumni Association's Senate and general chairman of marketing our beautiful coffee-table-type memory book for our college's sesquicentennial celebration in 1993. Also, I was elected chairman of the Alumni Athletic Advisory Committee and served on the Alumni Admissions Committee.

Marion and I became quite active together in genealogical research, beginning by taking a course in genealogy at the Brewster Mormon Church and then attending a two-week Elder Hostel class in research at Boston College. We both belong to the Cape Cod Genealogical Research Society, and I have been quite active in the sub-chapter dealing with doing research on Irish-

American ancestors. We have had good success in tracing back some of our ancestors, but it has been frustrating with others.

We have so far attended seven Elder Hostels in different parts of the United States and Canada: two in genealogy at Boston College; one on watercolor painting at Old Dominion University in Norfolk, Virginia; one at Western Carolina University in Waynesville, North Carolina, on art, golf, and current international affairs; one at Digby, Nova Scotia, Canada, on watercolor painting and the life of Joshua Slocum (the first man to circumnavigate the world all by himself); one in Tucson, Arizona, on southwestern United States art and culture; and one at Scarritt-Bennett College in Nashville, Tennessee, on Mozart, American classical movies, and influence of people on others. We are now looking ahead to our eighth Elder Hostel in the summer of 1996 on operating a computer, writing, nineteenth-century New England, or some other interesting subject. Elder Hostels have been a Godsend to us—traveling and meeting and sharing educational ideas with some wonderful new people, anywhere from age 50 to age 85, who are thirsty for new knowledge. We couldn't be more enthusiastic and would urge anyone who reads these memoirs to investigate attending upon reaching age 55.

Whenever we meet people from the town of Needham, the first question they ask us is, "Aren't you bored living on the Cape?" Nothing could be further from the truth. We've met some wonderful people in Brewster; we have traveled; we've experienced some new ventures and are extremely happy and satisfied with our life. God has been good to us both.   Now, with our new Apple computer and e-mail, we can correspond with our sons and their families in Seattle, Washington; Nashville, Tennessee; New York City; and Sudbury and Attleboro, Massachusetts. Whether our sons want to write us at midnight or two in the morning, they can always send an e-mail to us, and we can read it when we arise.

In August of 1995, Marion was awarded an honorary Bachelor of Fine Arts degree from the Art Institute of Boston, a graduate school of art that Marion had attended on a full-time basis after graduating from Emmanuel College in Boston with an A.B. in English. At that time, the Art Institute of Boston (then called Boston School of Art) was not a fully accredited four-year college with the authority to award bachelor of fine arts degrees. It received accreditation in only the early 1990s.

Once our five sons heard of this fine honor that was to be bestowed on their mother, they immediately decided to have a surprise dinner party for her on August 12, 1995, at the High Brewster Inn. Much secrecy was necessary to keep the event a surprise; however, everything went according to plan, and we had a wonderful evening. Our sons had engaged a professional photographer to take pictures of Marion and me and the five sons (see attached photo), and the diploma, beautifully framed, was presented to her.

On April 26, 1996, Marion was notified by the Brewster Board of Trade that she was going to be honored at a dinner on May 16, 1996, for her selection as the 1996 Brewster "Person of the Year." She was selected mainly for her over 1000 hours of volunteer work with the senior citizens of Brewster—giving of her talents and experience to help them with their art—but also for her untiring work as publicity chairman for the Brewster Historical Society, for her work with the Brewster Woman's Club, Our Lady of Cape Church Guild, and the Brewster Garden Club.

On December 8, 1996, Reverend Sean O'Malley, bishop of the Fall River Diocese, presented Marion with the prestigious Marian Award for outstanding service to Our Lady of the Cape Church in Brewster. Since I had had the honor of receiving this same medal in 1991, we became, to the best of our knowledge, the first couple in Our Lady of the Cape Church to receive the Marian Award.

EPILOGUE

In writing these memoirs, I have had the unique opportunity to review my past accomplishments as well as my past failures, my joys and my sorrows, my ecstasy and my agony, the 49 percent wrong decisions I have made in my lifetime (both in business and in domestic affairs) and the 51 percent right decisions, my married life with my beloved wife, Marion (how happy she has made me and how often I have let her down and disappointed her). How wonderful and forgiving the Good Lord has been to me over these almost four score years of life that I have been given.

Marion and I have been blessed with five wonderful sons who, like all of us humans, have had their failures and their successes. Both Marion and I feel that, all in all, they have turned out very well—mainly because of Marion's superb parenting, especially during their formative years when their character and basic values were being formed. Integrity, a strong sense of basic values, and a deep loyalty to their brothers, especially when one had a need—financial, social, or spiritual—have been quite evident in our five sons' everyday living. Actions speak much louder than words. Another strong characteristic Marion and I feel that our sons have is a deep commitment and devotion to their chosen careers. Mike, our oldest son, has been deeply interested and involved in the communications field since his years at Boston College High School, beginning with his period as co-editor-in-chief of the Year Book in 1967. Bill has shown his love and tender care of the retarded people he has cared for and with patients in nursing homes over his lifetime. David has had a strong commitment to the theater since his days as an actor in grammar school. Jack has been in love with computers and software since he took elective courses at Holy Cross, Clark University, and Worcester Tech in computers. Lastly, Joe has dedicated his life to the field of theater arts specializing in lighting design from his early days at Roxbury Latin School through Holy Cross and on to graduate work at the University of Virginia.

Our sons suffered through the trying days of the Vietnam conflict. Our three oldest sons were in college in those days and our two younger ones in high school or grade school. Marion and I suffered with them as we saw the inner conflicts they were having. Some of them wrestled with their faith and had a difficult time reconciling their feelings and those of the Church. All this time, Marion and I tried to "keep the door open" and prayed long and hard for them and their beliefs. We know that, with the help of God, they will realize how good God has been to them and how much He loves them and us all. May God be with them always and they with God.

In closing, I just want to stress the fact to our sons, to their good wives, and to our grandchildren, that Marion and I have tried our best, but we are certainly not error free, without sin or mistakes in judgment. We have made many mistakes in our lifetimes and will continue to err as long as we live. Remember: "To err is human, to forgive—divine." We have tried to make the right decisions. God has been good to us all. May He continue His love for us and we for HIM.

Ellen Starkey Saint - 1906

Brewster Bathing Beauties -1908

Ellen Saint and her Seven Children

Mary, Sarah, Thomas, Ellen, Alice, William, Peter, and Nell

Thomas E. Saint --1904

Ellen (Starkey) Saint,
Alice Saint, and her husband,G.. Knyvet Howes

Mary (Kelly) Saint -1912 - age 25

Saint's Rest -1924

Thomas E. Saint-1944-age 75-

Still active with Brown Durrell Co.

Paul F. Saint at Holy Cross Junior Prom-1939

Thomas A. Saint, George Cash, and Paul Saint

1St. Lt. Paul F. Saint
Italy-1943.

Thomas E. Saint, Paul F. Saint,USA

Paul and Marion Saint - 1995 With their five sons
Left to right:Joe,David,Mike,Bill, and Jack Saint

and
five grandchildren

Left to right:Michelle-1996-age five; Kaitlyn,1996-age two,

Amy-1996-age nine.

Molly Saint-1996-age four

Sarah Saint-1996-age two

It is quite a long time since we had a Saint family tree on the front page of the newsletter. It has been sent to us from America and is thought to go back to the early 1600's, originating in the U.K. with a Rogeri Saint; consequently a number of our readers will relate to it.

Please see the note about subscriptions in paragraph 950 of this newsletter.

Yours sincerely,

George W. Brown

939 continued

The family tree on the previous page was sent to us by Paul F. Saint of Brewster, Massachusetts, and is reconstructed from information researched by, and sent to him, by Mrs. Doreen Tout of Bristol. Mrs. Tout and the Editor feel that the period from John Saint b.1703 to John Saint baptised 1761 requires some verification and proof because John is quite a common name and there could be more than one person with that name in the area around that particular time. The earlier part

Because of its length the diagram has had to be split in two. The earlier part of the descent is shown below.

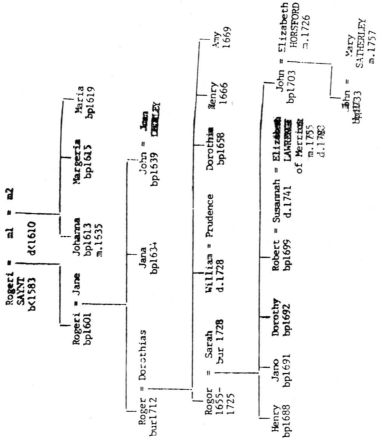

Rogeri Saynt was buried at Misterton, Somerset before 1642. His son Rogeri was baptised there in 1601 and grandson Roger who was buried in 1712 had been Clerk of the Parish for 30 years.

The Hearth Tax of June 1642 for Misterton showed Rogeri and John Saint, each with two chimneys, as 'none' payers. John Saint, brother of the Clerk, was a carpenter and carried out work on the church. Thomas, according to the Churchwardens Accounts, 'Keeper of the Fields 1642'.

John (1703) and Elizabeth Horsforth were married at Misterton in 1726. John Saint and Mary Satherley were married at Misterton on 6 June 1757.

939 PAUL F SAINT'S FAMILY TREE

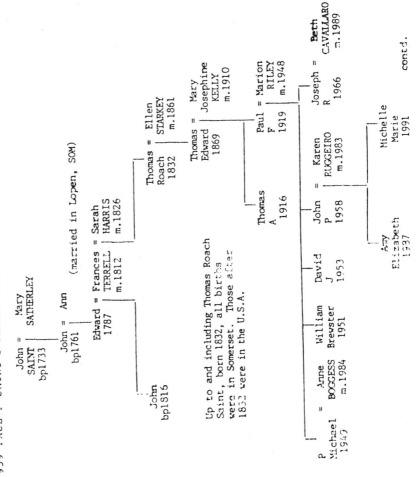

contd.